# BACKYARD TREEHOUSES

# BACKYARD TREEHOUSES

## Building Plans, Tips, and Advice

**DAN WRIGHT**

Guilford, Connecticut

An imprint of The Rowman & Littlefield Publishing Group, Inc.
4501 Forbes Blvd., Ste. 200
Lanham, MD 20706
www.rowman.com

Distributed by NATIONAL BOOK NETWORK

British Library Cataloguing in Publication Information available

**Library of Congress Cataloging-in-Publication Data available**

ISBN 978-1-4930-2985-3 (paperback)
ISBN 978-1-4930-2986-0 (e-book)

∞™ The paper used in this publication meets the minimum requirements of American National Standard for Information Sciences—Permanence of Paper for Printed Library Materials, ANSI/NISO Z39.48-1992.

Printed in the United States of America

# CONTENTS

# INTRODUCTION

I love sharing my passion for building in trees with other like-minded people. This craft of treehouse building is simultaneously art and science, arboriculture and carpentry, passion and work, engineering and philosophy. Paradoxical? Yes, but the pursuit of excellence is never one-dimensional.

I practice what I preach, too. Business may be both competition and collaboration, but I choose not to keep trade secrets. Collaboration leads us to better building, and so as much as I have benefitted professionally from treehouse builders before me, I am happy to share my unique contributions to the field.

You'll find that this book was not designed just to sell you our design or construction services. Yes, we're still in the business of supplying, designing, and building treehouses, but this book is 100 percent informational and was written with the goal of giving you what you need to do it yourself. I tell you how I approach the craft of treehouse building, and it is up to you to take what you want, leave what you don't, and determine for yourself what you are capable of building.

In the following pages let's dream together about what your treehouse adventure will look like. We'll follow our hearts for creativity, and use our heads to keep our trees happy and take us safely aloft.

Arboreal adventure awaits!

*Linda McManus Images*

# CHAPTER 1

# THE INSPIRATION, VISION, AND REASON FOR BUILDING A TREEHOUSE

Most of this book is about how to build the best possible treehouses. To start us off, however, we should spend some time considering why we build treehouses at all. The dreams in life that we believe in the most and work the hardest to realize usually have a strong reason behind them. And that reason drives us to complete the projects we start and to love them long afterward.

Treehouses are not generally considered essential for life. Most people do not use them as a primary home, but rather as a temporary getaway. Practically speaking, they are not the most efficient structures we can build. They are generally less energy efficient because the floor is exposed to variable weather. Treehouses take more time and money to build than an equivalently designed and outfitted ground house. Most kids grow up just fine without a treehouse in the backyard. In fact, many kids grow up just fine without a backyard at all. So what inspires us to build treehouses?

- Imagination
- Creativity
- Freedom or independence
- Escape from everyday life
- Nature
- Play
- Lucky kids (or lucky adults)

Treehouses reinforce life lessons.

Now we're getting warmer . . .

Treehouses create a sense of wonder in our hearts when we see them.
Even simple treehouses are amazing, not because of detailed construction
or expensive materials, but because of what treehouses represent to
us. When you build a treehouse, you share that wonder with everyone
around you. The kids are known at school as the kids with the really cool
treehouse. Throw wine and cheese parties on an arboreal perch connected
to your back deck by a rope bridge, and you are thought of as eccentric
and young-at-heart. And when Dad is sent out to the "doghouse"

(complete with a minifridge, a poker table, cable, and Wi-Fi), it just isn't all that bad anymore!

When parents take the time to build a treehouse with the kids, they are building relationships just as much as a physical structure. The treehouse becomes something the kids use for years and then later reminisce about as a place where they spent time with Mom, Dad, or their grandparents. When we spent two weeks building a treehouse for Sarah in Arlington, Virginia, it brought the entire neighborhood together. Even during an extremely divisive election cycle, Republicans and Democrats stopped to admire the project. A grandmother on her morning walk started to cry at the good memories it brought back for her. Treehouses create positive feelings that resonate deep in our souls. You just can't put a price on this.

## PERSPECTIVE

Our whole perspective on life changes when we sit in a tree. We're confidently doing something that mystifies most people who are stuck on the ground. As adults we can enjoy the breeze and swing in a hammock, releasing the cares of our workday. Something happens to kids when they get at least 6 feet into the air, too, because they become taller than adults and escape the reach of their parents and consequently feel greater freedom than just going to their room and shutting the door.

So, you see, what we are building is not just a structure in a tree. We are building memories, expressing creativity, connecting with nature, escaping from the confines of regular daily life, using our imagination, and realizing that every dream in this life is possible.

If I had a dollar for every time I got a call from somebody wanting me to finish a partially built treehouse, I wouldn't need to write this book. Starting a project is the easy part, because the desire is there. However, the full understanding of what it takes to finish the project does not always hit until you have started and realize that it's harder than it looks. Make sure that you have the right abilities and resources at the start so that you don't end up getting halfway there. My best advice to you? Start what you finish. Empower yourself.

One of the best ways to qualify yourself for the job is to attend a workshop. For example, I teach weekend-long treehouse-building workshops at least twice a year, which are part classroom learning and part hands-on experience (see Resources). These events attract DIY parents, architects, designers, carpenters, and future professional treehouse builders from all over the world. Our workshop graduates have started more than a dozen small treehouse-building companies and have built more than one hundred residential treehouses for their families. Some workshop participants, on the other hand, realize that they really aren't able to build their dream treehouse without help. We can then offer personal assistance with design, partial building, or full construction. If you aren't sure if you can do the job or finish what you start, then join us for a workshop, practice on our trees, and pick up some professional tips.

## REAL ESTATE

If you're building a treehouse, you're obviously going to need a tree. But even without a tree, you're going to need a spot of ground on which to root your project. It's a fanciful dream to carry wood, board by board, into a secluded spot inside a national or state forest and assemble a simple earthy treehouse to live in, but this usually does not end well. You might be sending a political message or feel good about your principles, but you will most certainly lose your treehouse in the end.

A common pitfall for landowners is to build the treehouse over the property line or within the building setback established by their town's zoning department. Both of these situations have led to treehouses being torn down at the owner's expense. If you are not absolutely sure where your property lines are, then consider hiring a surveyor. Whenever our clients have guessed or made incorrect assumptions about their property lines, it always leads to construction delays and unbudgeted expenses.

## TIME

If your treehouse is extremely simple, then you might be able to finish it in a weekend, but it almost always takes longer than planned. Building things at heights always takes longer due to the need for setting up ladders, scaffolding, and safety ropes. Weather can also cause delays. Those buddies who owe you a favor or said they would help for a case of beer may or may not come through as expected.

To reduce the time required to complete a project, consider renting or purchasing equipment such as rigging devices, scaffolding, and lifting machines to move lumber and lift walls. While these things aren't necessary, they will reduce construction time. Also, it's a good idea to have extra hands available to help, especially when you are working high in the air, as one person needs to stay on the ground to tie on and hoist up materials. We'll address these factors more in-depth in later chapters.

## COST

Whether the funds are coming from the piggy bank, a bonus from work, or a corporate fund-raising campaign, there is always a desire to get as much treehouse as possible for the money spent. Even when building a treehouse yourself, certain parts of the project will require some cash to complete. These include the following:

- **Hiring an arborist, engineer, or other expert.**
- **Permit fees, if applicable.** Check with your town's zoning and building departments.
- **Materials.** Even if some materials are reused or recycled, many of them will likely have to be purchased new.

- **Labor.** You might need more help than you can trade for beer. This especially applies if the treehouse requires electrical or plumbing work or any other specialized skill.
- **Accessories and furniture.** Don't let lack of budget force you to skip the fun finishing touches! Accessories are often the parts of the treehouse that get used the most over time. However, if you have to spread out the cost of a treehouse, the accessories are the easiest parts of the project to save for "phase 2."
- **Maintenance budget.** Make sure to take care of your trees and preserve exterior wood to get the most out of your project. Exterior wood also looks better when stained with an attractive color, which will have to be redone every three to eight years, depending on the surface type and application. As trees grow, every once in a while beams and joists may need adjustments. While this only happens every five to twenty years, depending on the tree's growth rate, it takes some money and time to keep the tree happy as the years fly by.

Life offers us countless ways to spend our time and resources. Some people should hire our company to design and deliver a turnkey project. Others should read this book or attend a workshop to learn the basics of treehouse construction and then build a treehouse themselves. And some who read this book will realize that they have misconceptions regarding the amount of time, cost, skill, trees, or other requirements for owning a treehouse, and therefore decide not to proceed with a treehouse at all. Instead of building a private treehouse, it may be better to visit public treehouses,

Big dreams and seed money

which are popping up all over the country at museums, arboretums, and city parks. We operate Treehouse World so that people who can't have a private treehouse on their property can come experience adventures in the trees like zip lining and climbing through unique treehouses. The purpose of this book, and of my life's work in this industry, is to help you—no matter who you are—to experience the excitement and adventure of the treehouse life.

Linda McManus Images

# INTRODUCTION TO CARPENTRY

**C**arpentry is the art and craft of building with wood. The basic skill sets are learned easily enough, but a lifetime can be spent gaining an intuitive sense of how to achieve the best results when framing, flooring,

Modern tools, ancient craft

trimming, carving, and bending. Wood must be harvested, milled, dried, cut, assembled, and finished. Each of these steps includes a skill set that takes years to develop. It may seem simple at first, but the more you practice the craft, the more you can appreciate a job well done.

Building a treehouse is carpentry come full circle, as it applies woodworking skills back to living trees. Special care should be given to preserve the life of the tree during construction, while building a structure that meets practical and aesthetic objectives to achieve a healthy, stable, and beautiful treehouse.

There is no need to master all carpentry techniques in order to build a treehouse, but the more you treat the project as an educational journey, the more you'll appreciate both the methods and your creation.

## WOOD

Each tree that is milled into lumber is cut to maximize the yield of the tree and generate dimensioned lumber. Most 6x6 and 4x4 is from the center of the tree and includes the pith that is visible on the end grain of the material. This part of the tree is used because posts are normally loaded

Each type of material is taken from a different part of the tree based on wood properties and intended use.

Examples of wood movement due to drying out

axially. However, joists and rafters such as 2x8, 2x10, and 2x12 are milled from the outer parts of the log, because the resulting grain orientation supports higher loading perpendicular to the board. Some hardwood floors are quarter-sawn to minimize expansion and contraction due to moisture changes. This practice helps the finished floor remain more stable over time.

When a tree is still alive and growing, the wood is moist and protected by physical and chemical barriers provided by the tree. When the tree dies, those protections start to wear down. When the tree is harvested, milled, dried, planed, transported, and stored, the wood undergoes many changes, but chief among them is that the wood dries out. This can change the shape and make it check, warp, cup, crown, or bow. That is why a wet board from the store may change shape when you take it home and stack it in the sun for an afternoon or two. If you want to paint or stain right away, or if you want to minimize the changes that wood goes through, then be sure the lumber is reasonably dry before you buy.

## "THE LOAD BEARING GENE"

A friend and fellow treehouse builder, Jake Jacobs, introduced me to the term "the load bearing gene" as a way to explain why some people build with a structural sense, and others just don't seem to get the basic principles of structural design. No, the Human Genome Project has not identified a gene for this yet, but I do notice that some of us have a natural propensity toward thoroughly logical building practices, while others of us repeatedly commit horrible jaw-dropping atrocities. These differences are often connected to our level of patience, standard of care, and motivations for building. Either way, if you get it, then please proceed with your project, as I'm not talking about you. If you read the following sections about loading and don't get it at all, however, then make sure you get some help with the structural elements of your treehouse project from somebody who does get it.

# ENGINEERING DEFINITIONS

**Dead Load:** The weight of all the permanent building materials and fixed accessories you place in the tree. Most treehouses have dead loads of 10 to 35 pounds/square foot.

**Live Load:** The weight of temporary loads. The primary live load is the total weight of the people who will use the structure. Live loads also include furniture or other transient items on a structure. In residential use, live loads are generally 25 to 40 pounds/square foot. In commercial use, loads might reach 100 pounds/square foot. You can sometimes use lower values for live loads when you can confidently restrict access to a set number of people or otherwise control maximum loading.

**Other Loads:** Snow loads, wind loads, seismic loads, and so on vary by area. Snow loads can be 0 in warm areas or 50 to 100 pounds/square foot in the North or up in the mountains. Wind loads are typically higher in the coastal areas affected by tropical storms than in inland areas.

**Total Load:** The sum of dead load, live load, and other loads that may be present simultaneously. For instance, if the treehouse is never used in winter, and the snow load does not exceed the live load, then the snow load can be ignored for design purposes.

**Safety Factor:** A multiplier to the total load intended to protect the structure during extreme conditions or account for loss of strength over time. Another reason to use a safety factor is to make sure that you can sleep at night, confident that the treehouse won't collapse. Safety factors normally range from 1.5 to 3 for structures and 5 to 15 for belay lines, zip lines, and dynamically loaded elements.

For example, if your treehouse is 10x10, then it is 100 square feet. If it's going in a residential backyard and you want to design to 40 pounds of live load per foot, then your live load is 4,000 pounds. The dead load could be about 1,500 pounds, depending on which materials you choose. If you only use the treehouse at your summer home and secure it from trespassers, then you can ignore snow loads. In this case your total load is 5,500 pounds. If you apply a 2x factor of safety, then you design the treehouse to 11,000 pounds. This is your total design load. Your total expected load is only 5,500 pounds, but you design it with a factor of safety for various reasons. The total design load must then be portioned out to each support point that could be a tree attachment bolt (TAB) or a post to the ground according to what percentage of the total load each support point carries. There are a host of variables that affect how much load each TAB will support in a tree, which we will cover later in this book. It depends on the tree as much as on the TAB. Also, it is critical not to assume that each TAB carries the same amount of load as the other TABs, because the beams, joist cantilevers, platform placement, and load-bearing wall locations all affect the proportional load path.

## MAKING STRUCTURAL DESIGN DECISIONS

Total design load is one of the first numbers to identify so you can decide on the types of tree attachments and ground supports to use. Structures are designed to withstand all expected loads, plus a safety factor. You never know exactly how much a structure weighs unless you can put it on a scale, so estimates are often used. Your lumber delivery company might be able to tell you the weight of your order if it is big enough to be the only order on the truck. Expected loads can also be calculated by lumber tables, or an engineer can make estimates based on tables for the type of construction you choose. If, right now, you are noticing that assumptions are made in this process, then, yes, you are correct. If each assumption is made conservatively, and a safety factor is used, then the chances of an accident are greatly reduced.

Proper material sizing is mostly about deflection under load. *Deflection* is the amount of "bounciness" a floor has when walked on. There are limits

# OAK LEAF PLATFORM AT TREEHOUSE WORLD

A very unusual treehouse, the Oak Leaf Platform at Treehouse World, demonstrates the range of deflection characteristics with parts of the platform exceeding normal levels by 3x (very stiff floor) and others being a bit more springy than you're used to. In order to support the long cantilevered lobes, extra solid blocking was required along with extra floor joists in some areas. The carpentry techniques required to make a platform with a deeply curved perimeter are advanced. If your carpentry ability is beginner level, then start with a rectangular shape. My favorite shape for a treehouse is a circle, but they are just so time-consuming to build that they aren't built very often.

Yoga camp at Treehouse World on the curved Oak Leaf Platform

for maximum deflection based on whether you are affixing drywall, plaster, or nothing to a ceiling. If you don't meet the deflection limit, the wood probably still won't break, but your plaster might crack from joists bending under normal loads, or the floor may sag under its own weight, which would make marbles roll to the middle of the room. Sizing a joist, rafter, stud, or beam is something you can pay an engineer to do for you. If you want the free version for smaller projects, then an experienced contractor or your local lumber yard sales rep may be able to assist you in sizing beams or joists for your project.

# A SINKING TREEHOUSE

One time, I was called in to fix a treehouse that was sinking. It had two beams that were 16 feet apart, and they were holding up 2x6 floor joists. Those probably should have been 2x12 joists. The floor was sinking under its own weight and was 4 inches low in the middle without anyone walking on it. It was so bouncy that it was scary for me to walk on. Our fix was to jack up the middle and set two posts in the ground with a beam down the middle to cut the joist span from 16 feet down to 8 feet, where 2x6 is acceptable.

If you do not feel confident making these decisions on your own, then there are a few options to get help:

1. Find a local structural engineer to design the treehouse.
2. Find a local carpenter who does design and build work.
3. Use our treehouse design services at treehousesupplies.com.

## PRINCIPLES OF LOADING IN ROOFS, WALLS, DECKS, AND TREES

Forces of all kinds will act upon your treehouse. The structure must be designed and built to resist excessive deflection, unwanted movement, or failure of any of the material components. Gravity, wind, growth of the tree, rain, and snow all will create various loading scenarios that must be accounted for during the design process.

## LOAD TRANSFERS

Loads caused by gravity must transfer down to the center of the Earth's mass. Inside a structure, the load passes through several materials along the way. For example, consider a heavy, wet snowfall from a record-setting nor'easter. The low back pain you endured after shoveling out of the last storm is a testament to how heavy snow can be. The load on the roof primarily flows down the rafters and onto the two bearing walls, where

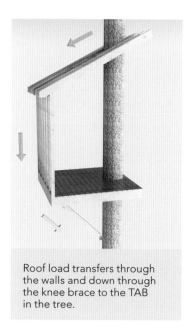

Roof load transfers through the walls and down through the knee brace to the TAB in the tree.

it is carried by the studs down to the floor. The floor joists then carry the load out to the nearest two beams, which then carry it to a TAB or a post to the ground. Each of these structural framing members must be sized to carry the loads that the structure is designed for. This is a highly organized way to design structures while minimizing the materials needed.

## GROUND CONNECTIONS: TREES VS. CONCRETE

In a typical ground house, a concrete footer is poured onto sufficiently hard ground and then floors or walls are erected on the hardened footer. Each spot along the footer carries some of the load and transfers it to the ground more or less evenly. Typically a joist or stud would sit on a sill plate every 16 inches. However, in treehouses the axial support structure is better thought of as a column or vertical cantilever than a foundation wall. If a beam is attached to two trees, then only those two columns transfer load to the ground. The beam must be sufficiently sized to carry each joist outward and set it on the two points. This language of point loads comes easily to those with a timber-frame background, but that is an old-fashioned art these days due to its reliance on increasingly rare heavy timbers and advancements in steel and engineered wood technology.

The tree column will sway a little in the wind, but it is unlikely to tip over if the tree's structural root zone is undamaged and if the tree is in a suitable environment. The yellow poplar (*Liriodendron tulipifera*) has a low incidence of uprooting when it grows in the middle to upland areas, but when it grows in the lowlands, such as near streams or floodplains, it can easily tip over when the soil is saturated and the wind blows. However, species

This oak tree blew over when the structural roots broke under tension.

like the bald cypress (*Taxodium distichum*) will grow well completely submerged. If a species is growing in an environment where it excels, and the individual specimen looks healthy with an absence of structural problems, then it is a good bet that the tree will adequately carry the load down the trunk and into the ground. A little research on the tree species is an important step at the beginning of the design phase of your project to make sure that you choose the best trees. The Internet, specifically state university forestry program sites, can provide information on most of the trees you will encounter. Alternatively, you can engage a tree professional such as an arborist or forester to help you identify your trees and tell you which ones look like the best bets for your treehouse.

## USING GROUND SUPPORT

Some people consider it inauthentic to use posts to the ground when supporting treehouses. However, many treehouse projects require

Holding a post plumb with temporary braces while stone or concrete is added

additional support. Other treehouses may start out being tree supported, only to have a tree die or be struck by lightning and require a ground post added to replace the tree. As a result, a treehouse builder needs to know how to use ground support as an option.

There are a few different schools of thought on post installation. The first one I learned was to dig a hole, set the post in the hole, and pour concrete around it. This tends to work out alright for pressure-treated poles. However, one of our engineers prefers that we use stone instead of concrete. The stone allows water to drain, which keeps the posts from

This cedar log rotted after about eight years underground.

For a more natural look, you can use a tree trunk instead of a treated 6x6.

These 12-foot-long utility poles are treated and much stronger than 6x6s.

Wires forming an X shape add stability to the posts.

## WOOD FOR GROUND CONTACT

Pressure-treated wood has many grades of treatment available. When wood is going to touch the ground, it should have the highest level of treatment and be labeled for ground contact. One alternative is to have ladder and stair treads rest on a stone instead of in the dirt.

rotting as quickly. Another method is to pour a footer that extends above grade and mount the post on top. The footer method results in the longest-lasting posts but provides no stability, which means that you will need reliable cross bracing made out of wood or tension wires.

## FLOOR LOADING

You will size your floor joists based on the largest distance they will span. If you have two parallel beams, the span may very well be equal all the way down. However, when incorporating three or more trees into a project, you are more likely to have a larger span

Ideally joists are parallel and 16 inches on center, but sometimes we must be creative to work around trees.

Joists are run at irregular angles to work around tree trunks in this spreading silver maple (*Acer saccharinum*).

at one side than the other. Use the floor joist size that is acceptable for the largest span distance.

The default layout for a floor is to install a joist every 16 inches on center. However, when multiple tree branches come up through the floor, you may have some joists that must be pieced in, or you might install the joists on unusual angles. Just maintain the joist spacing tight enough to support the decking. Common pressure-treated decking is best installed on joists that are kept close to the 16-inch spacing. Over 20 inches and standard flooring flexes noticeably more when you step between two joists. If you need or prefer to have joists spread farther than 16 inches apart on center, then one option is to use a stronger decking to span greater distances between adjacent floor joists. Expanding to a 2x6 decking instead of a ⅝x6, or switching to an engineered composite or a tropical hardwood, may allow

# CONSTRUCTION TIP

Sometimes you can stiffen up a slightly bouncy floor by adding a course of "solid bridging" down the middle. The blocks must be tight for it to work, and I recommend wood screws instead of nails to install them. When you step on one joist, the blocking helps share the load with the joist on either side, which reduces excess deflection. When installing joists 16 inches on center, the bridging pieces will mostly be 14.5 inches, which is often taken out of scrap pieces of wood after the common joists are installed.

Scraps of joists can be installed perpendicular and tight to increase floor strength.

you to space joists up to 24 inches. Check with the decking manufacturer or distributor for exact specifications.

## WALL LOADING

For single-story treehouses, 2x4 studs are generally sufficient for exterior and interior walls alike. We prefer a single bottom plate and a double top plate for walls. The double top plate helps lock opposing walls together before sheathing is applied and provides extra nailing for siding and rafters. Some exceptions to this rule of thumb are as follows:

- 2x3 may be sufficient for small structures, but often 2x3s are graded less carefully because they are more of a utility product. As a result, the cheaper 2x3s are often a bit more crooked, full of knots, or otherwise less easy to work with.

- 2x4 is too small for pocket doors, so you might need a 2x6 wall in those places.
- Thicker insulation may be desired for exterior walls in a climate-controlled treehouse, which could be a reason for a 2x6 exterior wall or a double 2x4 wall with offset studs.
- When adjoining walls are different heights, the second top plate can be omitted if desired. This happens with shed roof framing.

Framing around windows can be done a couple different ways. In conventional building you would use a king stud, jack stud, double 2x6 header (for typical window widths), and double sill plate. This allows extra nailing for interior and exterior trim and gives excellent protection to the window frame opening. However, many a simple backyard treehouse is OK with just a single layer of wood around window and door openings. I have seen many treehouses (and built some myself) with a simple window frame that are long-lasting. A strong siding material like T 1-11 plywood is usually enough to divert rafter loads around a window opening for a small treehouse. Also, when a rough opening is slightly bigger than the actual

Single-stud framing around these camp-style windows is sufficient for this project.

window, a very small amount of bending is OK before the window unit is stressed at all. And let's not forget that many treehouses don't use glass windows anyway, which means that it is OK to have some flexibility in the structure (and it reduces your material cost). One caveat: If you use only a single framing member around the window, you have to be careful that all of your nails and screws from siding and trim hit the narrow 1.5 inch of framing. For this reason I generally prefer a minimum of 3 inches of framing to make future steps easier and reduce exposed nail and screw tips.

## UNIQUE HOMEMADE WINDOWS AND DOORS

You can always go to the store and purchase a brand-new replacement or new construction window or door. If you do, you can expect standard, white, full size, with weather stripping included. If you are going to heat

Left: Closed shutter windows in a homemade frame
Right: Dutch door with separately hinged top and bottom

Secret back door with small landing

Homemade threshold beveled at 10 degrees to shed water outward

Door under loft leading to back exit

A small door that opens separately from the full door

Mini double door under loft

or air-condition your treehouse, then this is probably the way to go. Most exterior windows cost between $100 and $700, and most exterior doors cost between $300 and $1,000. Of course, you can spend more for custom-made stuff, but those are good ballparks to keep in mind.

When you build your own windows and doors, unless you are extremely talented and millwork is your hobby, you may find that it is challenging to make handles operate well, hinges that withstand a kid leaning on the door, thresholds that shed all rain outside the building envelope, or closures that keep the drafts out. If you don't mind taking on the challenge, then you can build some windows and doors with budgets of under $50 each.

## ROOF LOADING

Roof joists are called rafters, and they carry the roof load to the walls. Roof load comes from the weight of the roofing material, plus any rain, snow, or branches that fall onto it over the years.

The roof pitch means how steep the roof is. It is usually quoted as 4/12 or 6/12, and so on. The first number is the inches of rise, and the second number is always 12 for the standard inches of run. So 6/12 is steeper than 4/12 because it rises higher over the same run. In New Hampshire snow country, where I was born, most roofs on ground houses were in the 10/12 to 14/12 range. In Pennsylvania, where my company is now located, most roofs are about 8/12, which makes them cheaper to build and easier to walk on, but the snow piles up a little more on them. In the South you can find homes in the 2/12 to 6/12 range. Steeper-pitched roofs are not just about snow load: You might want to consider headroom if you are building a second story or a sleeping loft.

## FRAMING AROUND WINDOWS, SKYLIGHTS, AND TRAPDOORS

If you're installing a trapdoor, then you will need to cut one floor joist to make an opening large enough to climb through. Skylights may require

Header over a doorway

Header around a skylight

Headers around a trapdoor

Headers and sills around a window rough opening

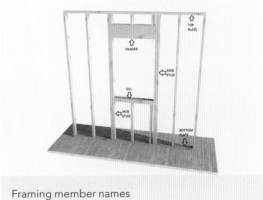

Framing member names

skipping a rafter or two. Large windows may require skipping studs. When this must be done, the opening shape is defined, and then headers are added to distribute load out to the nearest full framing boards. Then, extra boards are "sistered up" to replace the missing strength from the cut boards. This principle applies to floors, walls, and roofs whenever you need an opening that breaks the load path in the framing.

## PROPER USE OF FASTENERS

Nails and screws are about the same size, and both are used for joining pieces of wood, but they are designed to resist opposite types of forces. Screws are designed to resist tension or pulling out, whereas nails are designed for shear strength. It's not that you don't get some pullout resistance from nails and some shear strength from screws, but each was made for a distinct purpose. For example, have you ever seen an old deck where the nail heads are popping up? Screws are a better choice for decking if you don't want the fasteners to pull out as wood seasonally shrinks and expands. Nails are ideal fasteners for wall sheathing because the primary

| | | |
|---|---|---|
| | 2.5" GRK R4 Screw | Decking & Railings |
| | 3.125" GRK R4 Screw | Framing & Railings |
| | 4-10" GRK RSS Screws | Strong Timber Connections |
| | ½" x 7" Carriage Bolt | Railing Posts |
| | 1.75" Stainless Coil Nails | Siding & Cedar Shakes |
| | 1.25" Aluminum Coil Nails | Asphalt Shingles |
| | 3" Stick Nails | Framing |

Common fasteners used in treehouse building

function of sheathing is to hold the wall studs perfectly plumb and keep the wall square. Some fasteners are hybrids, such as ring-shanked nails with increased pullout resistance and timber bolt screws with increased shear strength. The important *safe building skill* is to choose the type of fastener most appropriate for its application.

In a typical backyard treehouse, I use the following:

1. Carriage bolts to connect posts to beams and railing posts to rim joists
2. TABs or custom tree attachment bolts to connect main supports to trees
3. Structural screws or small lag bolts to connect brackets to beams
4. 3-inch and 2.5-inch #10 screws for platform and wall framing
5. Stainless steel coil siding nails for many types of siding and roofing
6. Assortments of smaller screws and nails for building doors and trapdoors and installing windows and accessories
7. Many other product-specific fasteners, such as gasket screws for metal roofing, timber screws for beam connections, or hidden fastener systems for some types of decking material

## SAVING MONEY

There are many reasons to consider reusing materials for a treehouse, such as budget, design, longevity, availability, or philosophy. We design with reused materials whenever we can, although they don't always save money, they don't always have a low carbon footprint, and you still have to find an appropriate material for each specific purpose in the project.

Sometimes materials are available for free. With some basic salvaging skills, you may be able to save old windows or doors, wood, or metal panels that were destined for a landfill. Some playground equipment, especially slides, is thrown away long before its useful life is spent.

The major pitfall that I see in using old materials is that people tend to completely disregard the labor involved in using them. For example, finding a free set of old windows might seem great, until it takes four hours to scrape, paint, hinge, hang, and build jambs for each window. Depending on what your time is worth, you might find yourself wishing you bought new windows that come fully assembled and ready to plop into a rough opening. Also, keep in mind that the old window will not operate or insulate as smoothly as a new one, and it probably won't come with a screen. The same applies to doors, which can come prehung on jambs when purchased new.

If you decided to use old windows and doors, you'll only save money if you're doing the work yourself. I recommend going that route only if you really like the old windows you found and will appreciate them more than you would new ones.

Another downside to getting free materials is that you usually have to get them when they're available. This may mean moving them multiple times and having a place to store them until you are ready to build. All of us have an inner pack rat and think we'll eventually use anything, but what usually happens is we expand until all of the usable storage space is gone. We eventually have to throw a lot of things away that might otherwise be useful in other situations.

Free old wood might not have a lot of useful life left and may not be worth your time. But you can be selective here, too, because vertical siding boards might only be rotten on the bottom 2 feet, where water splashed up on them for years. If you can cut off the rotten part, then the tops may be in great condition. Or, the sunny side of an old barn might be weathered, but the other side has many years of life remaining. Many boards can be run lightly through a planer, then stained and given new life.

Aside from getting things free, you may be able to buy used materials from dealers. We frequent a local salvager in Coatesville, Pennsylvania, named Todd Waltz who takes down old barns for the siding and beams. The siding mostly gets milled into tongue-and-groove flooring, and the beams are either reused as beams or turned into fireplace mantels. The old-growth oak and pine that Todd is pulling out of Pennsylvania barns is hundreds of years old and has more character than anything on the market today.

Old-growth wood often can be salvaged from old barns or boats and repurposed.

However, you won't find this material to be inexpensive. It will cost more than new pine or oak boards. Other salvagers will keep yards of metal paneling or building materials to sell at below-new prices, but you usually have to be flexible on sizes and styles. Habitat for Humanity, for example, receives donated new and used building materials and then sells them cheaply to support their nonprofit organization. We have found some great deals on oddities like circle or elliptical windows, which would normally be slow-moving merchandise but is a prized find for a treehouse builder. You often can find rare things like stained-glass windows, decorations, and heavy doors at antiques shops, but be prepared to pay a premium, because these items are popular and the dealer often has to buy them at auction and mark them up to make a living. Lastly, you can review ads on message boards. We have found deals several times on Craigslist for things that we can use, but the quality in such places can be good or bad, so make sure you know what you're looking at.

Sometimes excess supplies can be turned into a bargain for you and also support a good cause.

## PRESERVING THE ENVIRONMENT

Reusing items wherever possible helps preserve the environment. Every reused board will decrease demand for a new board. Also, if the old materials were destined for a landfill, then you are reducing a pile of garbage somewhere. Wood will decay and return to soil quickly, but the more important materials to use as long as possible are plastics and glass. Aluminum and steel often get recycled anyway. Using old windows will save glass. The best plastic item to reuse is a slide. Most people use an outdoor swing set for about ten years and then throw the whole play set away, since used play sets have very little, if any, resale value. You should be able to get one for free. Plastic slides typically last a very long time.

If the environment is a high priority for you, then please keep in mind the environmental cost to get the materials delivered and ready for use. Some materials may need new paint. Others may need to be sanded, planed, or resized. Shipping, in itself, leaves a huge carbon footprint. One builder I know used old barn boards from Alaska, shipped to the West Coast, and then trucked across the country for use on a treehouse in Pennsylvania. I'm not trying to discourage you from saving the planet, but many well-intentioned people often overlook these factors in their efforts to be eco-friendly.

## MATCHING THE RIGHT MATERIALS

Some wood absolutely has to be in great shape. Beams, joists, and stair stringers immediately come to mind as places that you don't want to use partially decayed wood. Most of our projects use new pressure-treated lumber for these areas because that will last the longest. Other areas of the project can be changed in ten years if necessary, but rotten floor joists might mean a total rebuild of the treehouse. Great places to employ reused wood are siding, trim, and homemade doors. Decking and railings take a lot of abuse from the sun and rain, so I would reuse wood in these areas only if the wood is strong and solid as new.

Wood such as 2x4s and 2x6s for framing can sometimes be obtained from demolition sites. However, this is usually more trouble than it's worth. The wood can be very dry and is likely to split when using new nails or screws. It also may have holes or nails in it that need to be removed. It is certainly still safe to work with this material and can be worth it if you have a lot more time than money in your budget.

# CHAPTER 3

# INTRODUCTION TO TREES

Two basic questions will help you determine which trees are suitable to build in:

1.  Is the tree healthy?
2.  Is the tree strong?

Many trees are one but not the other. The healthiness of a tree is an assessment of its level of biological function. The strength of a tree is an assessment of the structural quality of its wood. A stump, or topped tree, is biologically dead, but the wood may remain structurally sound for a very long time, depending on the species and environment. Alternatively, a tree might be hollow and decaying on the inside but have leaves on every branch and be very much alive biologically on the outside. Seeing the tree independently through these two lenses will give you a complete picture of the overall suitability of any tree, regardless of species. All suitable trees for building treehouses will be healthy and free of major structural defects. In this section I explain what to look for during initial tree assessment and when to call for an expert arborist's help.

## BIOLOGY

The essential biological function of a tree is to use nutrients to create starch, which fuels structural growth, reproduction, and wound response mechanisms. Starches are also stored for later use and used by beneficial fungi that exist symbiotically underground. The level of starch production and use is the simplest way to describe the overall health and biological function of any tree. When trees are thriving biologically, they can grow to over 300 feet tall, over 20 feet thick, and live over 1,000 years. Granted, not all tree species have these capabilities, but each specimen has the potential to thrive as a prime example of what its species can become.

The environment where the tree is growing is primarily responsible for its biological success. Unfortunately for trees, they cannot walk around and find a better environment. They do their best with where they grow. Let's consider some environmental factors that help trees grow well.

## PICKING THE PERFECT TREE

There is no best tree species to build a treehouse in. Yes, some are better than others, but most trees are OK to use when they are good specimens and in a suitable environment. The Train Treehouse at Treehouse World uses two red oaks (*Quercus rubra*), two pignut hickories (*Carya glabra*), a Norway maple (*Acer platanoides*), and a cherry (*Prunus avium*). The cherry TABs had the lowest strength-test values, but all of the trees show excellent wound-wood formation. The train cars are all built like two-tree treehouses, and they are all unique in design. You can walk through each car, blow the real steam whistle, and take your picture in the engineer's window.

The Train Treehouse uses a variety of tree species and is 75 feet long.

## GOOD SOIL

There is no "one soil fits all" approach to trees. Some trees can tolerate different pH levels, soil structures, water saturation levels, or soil compositions. However, most of the research about soil has to do with planting new trees. The purpose of the studies is to identify which trees will thrive when planted in certain environments and for certain purposes.

For treehouses, we have a different question: Which trees are thriving in their current environment? We are considering established mature trees that have proven at least a minimum level of soil suitability. However, you should be looking for signs that the tree may not be firing on all cylinders, and if you see the signs, then it is most likely due to soil compaction or nutrient deficiency. People usually assume that if the tree looks unhealthy, then it has a pest killing it. Common pests include the emerald ash borer, hemlock woolly adelgid, pine bark beetle, and some others. However, you can locate the cause of most tree suffering by looking at the soil environment.

Poor soil environment will result in poor tree growth. Remember that trees need to move nutrients from the soil up to their leaves in order to grow. You may find that your tree has yellowish leaves in full summer. Compare the fullness of your tree's leaf canopy to other trees of the same species.

Look at the average leaf size or growth of shoots at the tips of a couple branches and compare these to other trees of similar age and species. Are all of the branches alive? A few dead branches on the inside of the tree canopy is usually normal as large trees mature, but if the outside of the canopy has a lot of small dead twigs at the outer

The right side of the tree is the natural state of a tree in the forest. The left side is debris piled too high against the trunk.

This picture shows old wounds from lawnmower damage. It's better to mulch these areas or trim them carefully.

branch tips, sometimes called perimeter "dieback" by arborists, then the recent growth of the tree is not going well.

When trees are suffering like this, it is most often due to root damage or soil compaction. Severing roots and compacting soil will decrease nutrient uptake, which can result in the low-vitality signs described earlier. Typically, root damage is due to changing the grade by adding or removing soil near the tree or by excavating for trenches, sidewalks, and swimming pools. However, it can also be due to mower or vehicle contact. Soil compaction is usually due to walking and driving on the soil. The compression reorganizes soil particles closer together, which removes air spaces. The lack of pores in the soil makes the soil drain slower, reduces gas exchange, and reduces the intake of nutrients from the soil. Try to avoid walking and driving on soil in general, but especially when the soil is wet, because soil structure becomes compacted more easily when particles are suspended in water.

Nutrient deficiencies can also restrict tree vitality, but it is often difficult to assess what's going on without taking soil samples and getting them tested in a lab. State university systems are often a good resource if you wish to test the soil. I do not recommend adding nutrients to soil or attempting to alter pH levels without first testing the soil. Fertilizing a tree before soil testing could not only be a waste of money and time but could actually make it worse.

Trees need soil with the right organic nutrients—specifically the "macronutrients" of nitrogen, phosphorus, potassium, magnesium, calcium, and sulfur. There are many other "micronutrients" that trees need in smaller

## A WORD ABOUT YARD LEAVES

The soil in places where all of the leaves are dutifully picked up every fall for decades can be nutrient deficient. In nature, fungi break leaves down and add the nutrients back into the soil. When leaves are removed, the soil changes. Fertilizer can help, although many fertilizers are deficient in many of the micronutrients that leaves and twigs contain. A good practice for long-

Mow right over the leaves for better tree health.

term soil management is to mow or mulch the leaves and "leaf" them where they lie, as long as you don't mind looking at them for a couple of months while they break down and enrich your soil.

amounts, such as iron, copper, chlorine, zinc, manganese, boron, and molybdenum.

## GOOD COMPETITIVE POSITION

It can be hard to get started as a little guy in this world. Every spring, we see the forest floor raise up little first- and second-year saplings, but very few of them reach maturity. In order to survive, a tree must collect nutrients from the ground, catch sunlight from the sky, deal with various conditions and variables, and hope for a healthy dose of luck. If a dozen trees grow close together, the ones that grow just a little taller will have a competitive edge in the sunlight contest. That will spur root growth, which will help them have an underground advantage as well.

Trees that compete for light will grow taller and have less taper. Trees that grow in the open by themselves will develop larger branches attached

This red oak (*Quercus rubrum*) tree has excellent positioning in the forest canopy and so is poised for growth.

lower on the trunk. The lower branches and increased taper will help the tree resist the higher wind forces out in the open. As a result, if a tree grows up in a forest, but nearby trees are cleared to make yard space, the tree can suddenly find itself with a narrowly tapered trunk and exposed to new wind forces, placing it at higher risk of wind damage.

When evaluating trees for positioning, look first at the shape of the crown as it relates to the forest canopy. Does the top of the tree get direct sunlight? Do branches on all sides of the tree get direct sunlight? Next, evaluate the spacing of the trunk to other trees in the area, which will give you an indication of how much the roots interfere with those of other trees. The closer together trees are, the more likely they are to compete in the structural root zone, have branches that rub against each other, and share the sunlight. The ideal tree to build a treehouse in will have average or better competitive positioning for sunlight and soil root space compared to all adjacent trees.

When two trunks grow close together, their crowns grow as if they are only one tree.

## ABSENCE OF BIOLOGICAL ATTACKERS

It is beyond the scope of this book to list the various beetles, aphids, scales, and bagworms that can hurt or kill trees. The emphasis here will be on recognizing any visible evidence that the tree is under attack and getting an expert arborist to assist in diagnosis when prudent. Many of the signs are the same as for root stress: discoloration, slow growth of shoots, small leaf size, and so on. However, some attackers also cause defoliation, leave exit holes in the bark, leave trails or nests visible on the trunk or leaves, or just reveal themselves by crawling around. If you see something unusual, you can research it or call in a professional to make sure that you do everything possible to pick a healthy tree and keep it healthy.

## STRUCTURE

Which came first, the trunk or the leaves? Well, the smallest of saplings are just small green shoots with a handful of regular-size leaves. Then in year two, they get a little taller, and the first year's growth starts to resemble wood. The seed contains some stored energy that fuels the original sprout. If conditions are good and those first few leaves collect some sunrays, then more starch is produced to fuel growth for a stronger structure and new leaves. If a deer notices the tender green shoots in the first couple years and nibbles them off, then the tree may run out of energy and die. Each year the biological function creates better structure, and that new structure supports new leaves higher in the air, which increase the next year's starch production.

Woody plants have a distinct advantage over nonwoody plants in the long run. Nonwoody material may grow faster initially, but the woody structure helps plants to support their chloroplasts higher in the air above nonwoody plants, and thus outcompete grasses and the like in the long run, not to mention they get out of the reach of deer, eventually. Trees even compete with each other, with some fast-growing species initially reaching canopy dominance, only to be overtaken by slower-growth trees that have better structure or evergreens that can keep photosynthesizing all year.

## CODOMINANT STEMS

Most treehouse trees have a centralized, or excurrent, structure. A central leader is the tallest and most dominant stem of the tree, and branches radiate outward on all sides. When inspecting the branch-to-trunk attachments, you want to see relatively small branches clearly enveloped by the vertical trunk. A rule of thumb is that branches are generally not more than about a third of the diameter of the trunk where the two join. Larger branches are likely competing with the leader for dominance. The most common structural problem with competing large branches is that the tree can develop included bark between the branch bark ridge and the trunk, which becomes a structural weak point. Such conditions are often called codominant stems. These are unreliable junctions in the tree, which lead to big splits or tear-outs during high-stress events like windstorms. Sometimes a weaker codominant stem can be reduced, which can improve tree structure over time.

The main branch does not form a ridge, but the second branch union higher up does.

The bump between the trunk and branch is the ridge, and the collar envelopes the branch beneath.

The crack between the two codominant stems has included bark and is prone to splitting.

This is an example of tree failure at the weak point created by included bark.

## HOLLOW TREES

Some hollow trees are still OK to use for treehouses, but consideration should be given to the extent of the dead tissue. Arborists generally recommend removal or reduction for trees that are over one-third hollow in the center. If the cavity is small and contained, then it will be less of an issue for the tree in the long run. However, conditions like butt rot, where the center of the tree is rotting from the ground upward, are likely to keep getting worse over time. This condition affects several of my scarlet oak and northern

An unusual swelling in the base of the tree could indicate basal decay.

red oak trees at Treehouse World, and I have made the decision to leave them and enjoy them a few more years, but not to invest in building treehouses in them, as they will eventually have to be removed.

Sometimes, while installing a TAB, you may encounter soft wood or discolored wood. It is important to note the depth and quality of the tree in order to assess whether the attachment point is still reliable to use. As we will discuss in future chapters, it is the wood on the outermost layers of the tree that is carrying most of the load of the treehouse, so if the back of the hole hits a contained hollow spot where a branch used to be, then this is not usually a significant concern. The age of the tree matters a lot. Younger and middle-aged trees will generally recover from early wounds. Mature trees have slower growth rates and are more susceptible to spreading wood decay.

## STRUCTURAL ROOT ZONE

Absorbing roots of large trees may extend 100 to 200 feet away from the trunk, but most of the structural roots that are anchoring the tree are within the top 3 feet of soil and within about 6 to 15 feet from the trunk. These are the roots that keep a tree from blowing over. Look at the roots where they start to turn horizontal and dive underground. Make sure that there are no girdling roots or major root flares that are dead or severely damaged. This is often caused when construction equipment bumps trees or digs trenches tangential to the tree trunk.

These two small trees should be cut to benefit the large white pine (*Pinus strobus*), but the rock should stay where it is.

The path on the right was cut and rocks placed on the left. This tree could die from this damage.

A tree should generally not have material packed up against the trunk. This happens a lot with new plantings that get volcano mulched or buried too deeply. Root crown clearing is a good idea in these cases. However, in the woods, a root crown clearing is usually unnecessary, as trees tend to grow at the proper height. If you do find excess material such as logs or big rocks touching the trunk, then you should pull them away as long as you don't cause further damage to the tree. For example, if the tree trunk is already growing around a rock, then removing the rock might open a wound in the tree. In this case it would be better to leave the rock. With trees like coastal redwoods that naturally drop leaf piles around their trunks and the material naturally builds up, there is no need to dig it all away unless there is another good reason for a root inspection.

## TREE WOUNDS

Being a treehouse builder, arborist, and all-around expert on things built in trees (or "tree geek" for short), I pay a lot of attention to the way trees respond over time to various types of structural damage. I have seen trees wounded from natural causes, like storms and animal rubs, and wounds from people, like lawnmower strikes, carved initials, deer stands, nails and hooks, pruning cuts, and, of course, TABs and other treehouse-building methods. Understanding wound response in trees could be the single most important bit of theoretical knowledge you take away from reading this book, as it will affect how you work in and around your trees.

## Trees Don't Heal, They Seal!

When something cuts human skin, the body grows new cells to replace the damaged cells. Old, damaged cells are removed by the circulatory system. Trees, however, do not remove or replace damaged cells, but rather they seal them off chemically and add additional structural tissue around the wounds that compensates for the initial lack of strength. As a result, any wound on a tree will remain for the lifespan of the tree. Typically, the new compensatory growth (often called *callus tissue*) closes around a wound from the left and right sides of a wound before it does around the top and bottom. The reason this occurs in this pattern is that the tree's circulatory system comprises elongated cells that connect vertically end to end, forming strings of cells. The sides of the wound are closer to unbroken strings of cells, which

### CODIT

Dr. Alex Shigo had a unique approach to studying trees. He cut them up and studied them from the inside out. He developed a model for compartmentalization of decay in trees, or CODIT. The trees tend to seal off wounds in patterns. His four walls of compartmentalization are 1) vertical spread, 2) circumferential spread, 3) inward spread, and 4) outward spread. Wall 1 is the first to fail, the last to seal with callus tissue, and the most important for bearing most loads associated with treehouse building.

This is a six-year-old TAB installation completely sealed. Chestnut oak (*Quercus montana*).

Callus tissue races against decay zone deterioration. Sugar maple (*Acer saccharum*).

Two-year-old TAB in eastern hemlock (*Tsuga canadensis*)

allow for a faster supply of starches and therefore faster growth of callus tissue.

## THE RACE

Wounded tree tissue in an otherwise healthy tree is immediately sealed off from the rest of the organism. The area that gets sealed off immediately starts to decay, so we can call it the *decay zone*. Wood decay rates vary greatly. Some trees will rot and become nonstructural in a matter of a couple years, while others will last multiple decades before becoming nonstructural. I use the term "nonstructural" to indicate that the wood becomes so soft that if a TAB is bearing on it, the load from the treehouse will eventually push the TAB downward through the decayed wood. As the decay zone deteriorates, the tree adds new growth rings each year and adds callus tissue around the wounded area, which bolsters the TAB and holds it secure in new healthy tissues. The "race" is whether the tree can add sufficient tissue after the installation before the decay zone becomes nonstructural. Of course, I cannot offer blanket statements about timing and predictions. Tree species, age, shape, and overall vitality are the most important factors that affect decay rates and rates of callus tissue formation.

## PRUNING

Trees are generally best left alone by humans. However, when we decide to prune tree branches, there are definitely right and wrong ways to do it.

### How Much Is OK to Prune?

Every leaf-carrying branch removed will reduce the total photosynthesis of the tree in subsequent years. You don't want to reduce this at all, because you want the tree to have a strong reaction growth response to the bolts that will hold up your treehouse. However, a small amount of pruning may be required for the project. Arborists try not to prune more than 10 percent of the leaf crown of a very mature tree, because the older the tree gets, the more it has to use all available energy just to maintain its structure. Younger trees are using a higher percentage for growth, so it might be OK in some situations to prune 20 to 30 percent of younger to middle-aged trees.

## Which Branches Should Be Pruned?

The best situation for the tree is to prune any dead wood you want, but minimize the cutting of live branches, as this harms the tree. In some cases, however, pruning live branches can make construction a lot easier or open up a majestic view from the finished treehouse. I have also learned that kids and visitors are not always nice to small branches, so if a small branch is in reach, then it might get damaged by the end users of the treehouse anyway. In those cases where I suspect damage will occur, I prune the branches cleanly to prevent larger wounds such as tear-outs.

## How Should Branches Be Pruned?

The best pruning cuts are clean and do not cut into the tissue of the next major branch or the trunk. Generally a reduction cut is made back to a

The final pruning cut should be outside of the bark ridge above and branch collar below so as not to damage the trunk tissues.

point where the new terminal has at least one-third the diameter of the part that is cut, which will improve the chances of the new terminal having a high enough growth rate to effectively take over and save the branch. When a large branch is removed, it is best to take it out in sections. First, remove the majority of the weight of the branch, and then go close to the trunk and make a clean cut just outside the bark ridge above and branch collar underneath. This is different than a flush cut, which exposes the tissue of the trunk to decay. It may look like you are leaving a bump where the branch used to be, but that is the proper way to prune if you want the tree to recover well.

# CHAPTER 4

# THE FIVE PRIMARY WAYS TO ATTACH TO TREES

Throughout this chapter, we will evaluate various tree attachment methods according to two criteria: (1) how reliably strong the method is, and (2) what impact it has on tree health. The best methods of tree attachment provide sufficient strength to keep people safe while minimizing tree impact.

The question of strength must be considered in both the short and long term. We must assess how long materials are expected to last outdoors in the sun and rain. Ultimately, it is the strength of the structure that keeps people safe, so a reliable attachment is of paramount importance.

The impact on tree health usually is a mostly qualitative assessment of how much initial damage is done to the tree (predrilling of holes) and how much of the tree's future growth will be affected by interference of materials touching the bark. We will refer to growth interference and initial damage in each section that follows.

## PIN VS. PERCH

The most common way that most bad treehouse plans suggest attaching to trees is what I call a pin attachment. You will find dozens of plans that teach this method, and it has pros and cons.

Board lag bolted to trunk

A pin attachment is where a wooden beam or joist is set flat against the tree bark and bolted or screwed directly into the tree. When an object touches a tree, one of two things will happen: The tree will envelop the object or push it away as the tree grows. When a structural beam is pinned to the tree, either option eventually leads to an unacceptable result. One way stunts the growth and structure of the tree; the other way results in a beam that eventually detaches from the bolt in the tree. The main reason not to use this method is that the growth interference is high and gets worse each year. Living trees add new growth each year, which makes every trunk and branch add girth.

There are three advantages to the pin method: 1) easier installation, 2) lower fastener cost, and 3) smaller initial pilot hole sizes. These are all meaningful

## TREE ATTACHMENTS

Trees either envelop or push away whatever is attached to them. If small screws or bolts without washers are used, then the tree may push a pinned board off the head of the bolt. However, if the fastener has a large washer, the tree may not have enough force to push it away and instead grow around it as best it can. Many poorly built treehouses need repair in only three to five years because the main beams become insecure.

Tree pushing boards outward as it grows

advantages to some people. As a result, many people with lower budgets and less skill will not follow much of the advice in this book. However, it isn't just my opinion that this is a bad trade-off. The treehouse industry is in general agreement that TABs or TAB-like fastening systems that function like artificial tree limbs (not a perfect analogy, but it is

Tree pushing board over bolt head. New bolt was installed afterward.

somewhat useful) are the best method for attaching medium to larger loads on trees that are intended for medium- to long-term project durations. However, TABs are a custom part that you have to buy from a company like mine (treehousesupplies.com), and they are not cheap to produce. They require a multistep drilling process, which is more difficult but totally possible once you watch the free installation videos on our website.

A perched load is where a TAB or similarly designed system is installed into the tree and the beam rests (typically) on top of the TAB a few inches away from the tree. The only part of the treehouse that touches the

tree is the TAB itself, which allows the tree to continue to grow outward over time. This method also preserves the tree's natural structure in the long run and allows for more uniform stress over the entire organism. The perched load method has a slightly higher initial impact on the tree due to the larger predrilled hole, but

Beam is perched 2 inches away from the tree trunk.

# TREE ATTACHMENT BOLT (TAB) INSTALLATION

The TAB is best installed with a few specific but available tools and drill bits. Start with a right-angle drill that turns with high torque and low speed. We have used several brands of this type of drill with success. Using a common smaller drill runs the risk of damaging the drill motor, especially if you're installing in a dense hardwood tree. Start with the 3-inch timber bit drilling to the depth of the collar on the TAB. Next use a 1$\frac{1}{8}$-inch ship auger bit to drill the second stage, and then a 1-inch ship auger bit to drill the last stage to the full depth. These three bits are sometimes on the shelf, but we can also supply them to you. Once

Start the hole with a 3-inch timber bit.

Turn the TAB into the tree using ropes for safety and positioning.

the hole is predrilled, the TAB can be started by hand, then finished with a ¾-inch drive socket wrench. You might need to add a pipe for leverage near the end. Please see the installation videos at treehousesupplies.com for more thorough instructions.

**Pro Tip:** The nut can be tight on the TAB once turned in, so try to remember to put the steel bracket on the TAB before turning it into the tree! Otherwise you may need a large pipe wrench, a bandsaw, or heat to remove the nut.

the growth interference gets smaller over time as a percentage of the total circumference of the tree. That is why the TAB is the standard attachment system for treehouses when you want the tree and the treehouse to last five to ten years or more. Asking a pinned beam structure to last that long is not good for the tree or the structure. So in summary, the optimal attachment method comes down to your anticipated project lifespan and how much you value the long-term health of the tree.

## Brackets

Various brackets are available to connect the beams to the TAB. Floating brackets allow the trees to sway without stressing the structure. Fixed

A slotted bracket allows trees to sway in any direction.

A fixed "pipe bracket"

Single knee brace brackets support the perimeter of a platform.

Single knee brace bracket

Double knee brace bracket secures two braces to a single TAB.

Forty-five-degree angle brackets used for suspension

brackets rigidly attach the beams to the TABs and do not allow movement. Other brackets are designed to mount to knee braces and inverted truss

## A WORD ABOUT TABS

Without going into all of the details, some of which are proprietary to our company, TABs are produced by a quality-oriented machine shop in the USA and go through a precise regimen of machining, heat treating, and normalization to make them suitable for real-world conditions involving constant cyclical stresses. The design specifications have allowed our treehouses to withstand hurricanes from Texas to Florida to New Jersey. Strong storms whip the trees around and shift loads from one TAB to another. A lot of thought went into the design and improvement of these parts, and we are very proud of them.

(tribeam) arrangements, to hang cables from, or to connect to suspension plates. Every year we come up with new ideas and create new brackets for custom projects as needed. However, over 90 percent of what we use for typical treehouse projects are the tried-and-true systems that are available on our website (treehousesupplies.com) and shown here.

Suspension plates allow reinforcement of the TAB under high loads.

## BOLT VS. WRAP

Is it better to bolt through a tree or wrap around it? This is one of the most debated questions at conferences for treehouse and challenge-course builders. The question is usually asked in regard to applications that create tension load or sideways pulling load on the tree trunk, such as a wire for a zip line, tension bridge, or challenge course element. Arborists can reasonably disagree on the matter, so you won't find a black-and-white answer here. I use both in my construction practice in different applications. There are pros and cons to each method, so we will discuss each in turn, and you can decide which makes the most sense to you for your situation.

Two zip lines attached with slings

## Bolting to Trees

Most bolting for large loads and loads critical to maintaining safety is done with through bolts that pass completely through the tree and have a washer and nut on the far side. The bolts commonly have eyelets or built-in thimble eyelets on the front side that are made for attaching wires or other hardware, such as a shackle or turnbuckle.

To install a through bolt, drill a hole through the tree that is the same size or $\frac{1}{16}$ inch bigger than the diameter of the bolt. The bolt does not thread into the tree, so push or tap it through and then thread a washer and nut on the back side.

## HELPFUL TIPS

**Tip One:** Use a structural washer to ensure that the washer does not implode or deform in any way when a force pulls on the front of the bolt. That washer is the only thing keeping the bolt from pulling through the tree.

Structural washers are larger and stronger than normal flat washers.

**Tip Two:** Install extra standard washers and nuts on the end of the bolt. As the tree grows and envelops the first nut, you don't have to worry whether the inside of the tree is decaying, because you can see your second or third washer is seated outside of solid wood. That's an extra level of safety that costs less than a dollar.

Extra washer and nut added to allow inspection after tree growth

# LAG BOLTS VS. THROUGH BOLTS

Through bolts transfer the load completely through to the back side of the tree. The washer and nut transfer the load from the bolt to the outside of the tree. However, lag bolts or lag screws transfer the load to the center of the tree, as each thread screws behind a layer of tree tissue. As long as the tree tissue does not decay and become soft, a lag screw will remain a reliable fastener. However, because

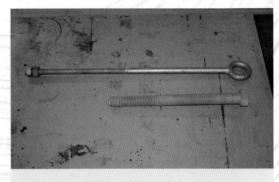

Large through bolt and lag bolt

the inside of a tree is not easily inspected over time, lag screws are best avoided in critical applications where a failure could lead to serious injury.

The benefits of bolting include the following:

- Bolts remain in a fixed position, which eliminates variables and prevents rubbing against the tree.
- Galvanized bolts resist weathering.
- Bolts with a ⅝-inch and greater diameter are reliable for a long time, although in commercial environments, standards dictate adding a backup wire in case of bolt failure. Bolt failure is very unlikely, but if you can't see inside the tree, then you can't be sure that the rod portion of the bolt remains in good condition.

Bolted zip lines eventually get overgrown and need to be rebolted.

Backup wires, common in the challenge course industry, are prone to girdle trees.

The drawbacks to bolting include the following:

- A hole must be drilled in the tree, causing initial damage.
- As the tree grows, you may eventually have to "rebolt" or install a second bolt and transfer the load to maintain safety.

## Wrapping Around Trees

The two major ways to wrap around a tree are direct wrapping and using a sling. We mostly use slings in our business because it is a cleaner look and easy on tree bark. However, when I see work completed by others, I notice they almost always directly wrap the end of the wire around the tree, sometimes up to four loops, and then cable clamp or eye termination with a quick link onto the live end of the wire.

Wide straps are a good tree attachment for zip lines and other tension loads. This 4-inch strap is in basket formation and so is rated at 25,000 pounds. Of course, UV rays break the material down, which is why we periodically test and change them according to our operations manual. This is the landing of the first zip line at Treehouse World, approximately 30 feet high in a large walnut tree (*Juglans nigra*).

Wrap method for tension loads on a tree

## Wrapping with Slings

Slings are wrapped one time around the tree and the ends joined together facing the direction of the wire pull. This is called the basket configuration, which yields the highest load ratings unless the two ends are brought together tightly around the tree, forming a large, obtuse angle where they join. As a rule of thumb, I want the two ends to join each other at 60 degrees or less, which is only about a 14 percent reduction from the true 90-degree basket strength. The smaller the angle, the smaller the reduction.

## Wrapping with Wire Rope

Most challenge courses run belay lines from tree to tree, with each end of the wire rope wrapped around the trunk a few times and then reattached to itself. The big risk is that if the wire is tightly attached around the tree trunk, the tree trunk will not have space to grow outward. You may see

Wooden blocks are temporary protection, but they must be adjusted over time as needed.

bulges start to develop around the wires that will eventually compromise the structural integrity of the tree at best, and can kill the tree in a matter of a few years at worst. A minimum step to take would be to put something between the tree and the wires, such as a series of vertical blocks of wood such as 4x4s. You will need about ten blocks to go around a 24-inch diameter tree and keep the wires from touching the trunk in between the blocks.

The benefits of wrapping with slings include the following:

- No significant tree damage, as no blocking is nailed into the tree.
- All parts of the system are visible for inspection.
- A wide sling does not girdle trees and will expand as the tree grows.
- Slings are very strong when new.

The drawback of wrapping with slings is that slings need to be inspected and replaced periodically due to UV exposure, wear, and animal damage.

The benefits of wrapping with wire rope include the following:

- Only small nail/screw holes are made during installation.
- All parts of the system are visible for inspection.
- Wire is reliable and will last longer than a synthetic sling outdoors.
- Blocks of wood or other materials can be installed to prevent tree girdling.

Wires wrapped around a tree can eventually kill the tree by constricting its transport systems.

The drawback of wrapping with wire rope is that in order to adequately prevent tree girdling, the tree needs to be attended to and the wrapping redone periodically due to tree growth and grooves that wear in the blocks.

## POSTS VS. EVERYTHING ELSE

Ground support for treehouses is normally in the form of a wooden or metal post from a concrete footing in the ground up to a beam. If a treehouse is entirely on posts, it may look like other elevated buildings, such as a boathouse on the ocean, a fire watch tower, or a home built in an area that floods. For these types of projects, you can follow general building conventions in your area that apply to:

- Types of footings acceptable for the ground conditions;
- Footer depth to be below the frost line;
- Pole length and diameter.

Most of our projects that use ground support are actually hybrid structures that attach to trees and use posts for additional support. This usually happens when people want a very large treehouse but only have small to medium-size trees or don't have enough healthy trees to carry the project. With a little bit of vision and creativity, hybrid structures can be designed and built in a way that doesn't lose the feeling of an authentic treehouse.

## MASTER/SLAVE DESIGN IN HYBRID TREEHOUSES

The chief structural issue with hybrid treehouses is that the trees sway back and forth, while posts generally do not. My preferred design is to consider all posts fixed-support points, or "the master." Let's ignore that wooden posts without cross bracing actually do bend a little bit and just assume that they are in a fixed position on a solid footing. All of the trees are outfitted either with floating brackets on TABs or with a suspended chain or wire rope system from a TAB 2 feet to 6 feet higher in the tree. This allows for a small amount of tree movement without pulling the structure laterally. In this configuration the trees are the slaves. The platform and treehouse remain still and fixed to the posts.

The floating bracket has a slot in it and is permanently screwed into the underside of a beam, so the bracket stays still with the treehouse. The TAB, however, is permanently installed into the tree, so the TAB moves with the tree. The TAB sticks through the slot of the floating bracket, which carries the load of the treehouse. But the bracket can slide around, up to a couple inches in any direction. In this fashion the tree is free to sway whichever way the wind blows without moving the treehouse.

Trees move more in the middle and top than near the ground. A solid, sturdy trunk may only move an inch at 12 feet high even in high winds. Of course, actual movement distance depends on species, size, and environment. However, the constant is that the closer your treehouse is to the ground, the less of an issue tree movement will be. It is very challenging and therefore very unusual to build large treehouses that are over 20 feet high, because tree movement becomes a much bigger challenge.

# CHAPTER 5

# COMMON TREEHOUSE PLANS

## TIPS FOR ALL PLANS

The plans in this section are kept rather general because every tree and set of trees is different. Trees that are 16 feet apart will require a much larger beam than trees only 10 feet apart. So my focus is on the basic approaches of how to properly attach to trees for common backyard treehouse designs. I deliberately avoid some of the specific details which you will likely have to adjust to the tree spacing that you are working with. However, our treehouse supply store will help you if you get stumped on any specifics. You also may be able to get some basic suggestions from the lumber yard that you plan to order from. They often have charts and can help you pick the best beam sizes if you bring them measurements of your trees.

## Material Takeoff Suggestions

**Beams:** Custom measure and estimation of loads

**Joists:** For 16 inches on center, you have a joist on the start, and then add 3 more joists for every 4 feet of platform. So a 12-foot-wide platform needs 1 + 3 + 3 + 3 = 10 common joists. Don't forget to add 2 joists for the rim joists, and extra if you need headers for framing trapdoors or working around tree limbs.

**Decking:** Generally decking is sold as 8-foot, 10-foot, 12-foot, or 16-foot pieces. 5/4x6 is the most common board, and it is usually 5.5 inches wide, but with a small space between boards, plan on each board covering 5.625

inches. So if the deck is 8 feet, then divide 96 inches by 5.625 inches and get 17.06 boards. I would round down and buy 17 boards, and ignore the extra ¹⁄₁₆-inch remainder on the end.

**Wall studs:** Depending on the complexity of the treehouse, we usually need about 1.4 to 2 studs per lineal foot of wall. For example, a 10x10 treehouse has a perimeter of 40 feet. So my initial order would include between 52 and 80 studs for the wall, depending on how many windows, complex openings like bay windows, or other specifics of the design.

**Siding:** Plywood or T 1-11 is sold in 4x8 sheets and you just count them. However, wood siding is sold by the lineal foot, and you need to calculate the coverage. I suggest buying 5–10 percent extra for stable boards that are nearly all usable condition. However, if getting reclaimed lumber, rough-sawn or live-edge siding, I suggest buying 15–20 percent extra, as more pieces will be rejected and you may want to be more selective about appearances of those materials.

## Setting Level

A regular spirit level or line level will work for some designs. Other methods will help when you don't have a direct line of sight between each TAB location. To get multiple TABs on opposite sides of a tree installed perfectly level, you can set up a transit or rotary laser far away from the tree. We generally use a water level, which is a clear plastic tube filled with water. The water level is problematic when it's cold enough to freeze or over great distances. However, if you let all of the air bubbles escape first, then it is extremely accurate.

## Installing Tree Attachment Bolts (TABs)

Installing TABs requires a careful eye, some muscle, the right tools, and making no mistakes. Out of respect for the tree, if you drill a hole in the wrong spot, then you find a way to use the bolt in that spot. So measure twice and don't make mistakes here.

Use a "hole hawg"–style drill, which is right-angle oriented and produces very high torque at low speeds. This is very important, as I have burned out the motors on several smaller ½-inch chuck drills of various brand names. However, the right drill will install hundreds of TABs in trees. I recommend a two-step drill process. The first step is done with a 3-inch timber bit. Hold the drill level, checking with a small torpedo or line level on top of the drill head, and start the hole by pulsing the trigger until you get the feel of it. Drill the timber bit to the desired depth based on the size of the TAB. The second step is done with a 1⅛-inch ship auger that is at least a foot long. Put the bit in the center pilot mark left by the first bit, level, center the bit left to right, and drill 6¼ inches deeper into the tree. I suggest only drilling 1 to 2 inches at a time to ensure that you clear the wood chips properly and don't get the drill bit stuck. In extremely dense trees, this tip is essential.

## TAB Size

We use various sizes of TABs depending on the weight of the treehouse we are going to build and the hardness of the tree species we are working in. The 1x6 TAB was the industry standard for several years in the early 2000s. However, we moved toward making more of the 3x9s and 6x12s because they will support many times more load without bending or crushing tree tissue under the collars or bending under loads.

My treehouse store has eight sizes available at any given time. However, the common sizes that get used the most are 1x6, 1x9, 3x9, and 6x12. The first number (1, 3, or 6) is the length of the "collar." The collar is also sometimes referred to as the "boss." The collar is the 3-inch-thick part of the TAB that is bearing on the structural tree tissues (xylem). The second number (6, 9, or 12) is the length of TAB "perch," which extends outward past the collar. The brackets for all standard TABs are made to attach to the perch.

We load test occasionally as required by engineering. One project last year involved a pignut hickory (*Carya glabra*), a black oak (*Quercus velutina*), and a Norway maple (*Acer platanoides*). We used a 6x12 TAB in each tree. The hickory supported 7,300 pounds, the oak 8,200 pounds, and the maple 4,400 pounds. Most of this difference could be explained by the density range of each tree species. However, age, growing conditions, and general variability do apply, so I don't produce charts for TAB sizing. If you have doubts about which size TAB to use, then either hire an engineer or contact my supply store for advice before you make your purchase.

# PLAN #1: ONE TREE, TWO POSTS

## Stage 1

Install one TAB 3x9 bolt and pipe bracket at desired height in the tree for the top of the tribeam. Be sure to have your pipe bracket on

the TAB before you turn it into the tree.

(See the video on installing TABs at Treehousesupplies.com.)

## Stage 2

Build the tribeam on the ground and then, with help, lift and attach it to the pipe bracket located on the top TAB bolt. A rope and pulley system makes this easier to lift, especially when building out of easy reach. Once it is in place, hold the top part of the tribeam level, and then mark the location for the bottom TAB through the hole in the bracket at the bottom of the tribeam. Drill for the bottom TAB, but we suggest tilting the tribeam and inserting the bottom TAB into the bracket before turning the TAB into the tree. We can usually put this TAB in the tree without disconnecting the Tribeam from the upper TAB and bracket.

(See the video on building tribeams at Treehousesupplies .com.)

## Stage 3

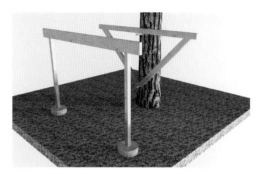

Lay out and build your concrete footings to support the 6x6 posts and beam. Carefully use a laser, water level, or regular spirit level to notch the posts for the beam to ensure that the top of the tribeam is level with the top of the beam on the two posts. Important: Check your local codes to determine footing size/depth. For a 10x10 single-story treehouse, a double 2x12 beam should be sufficient, or a double 2x8 beam with properly connected angle braces to shorten the span.

## Stage 4

Next, cut all joists on ground and attach them to your beam and tribeam. We suggest screwing the joists in place instead of nailing so that if they need to be shifted, they will be easier to modify. I advise leaving 3 to 6 inches of space between joists and the tree to minimize future maintenance as the tree grows. If needed, use temporary bracing on the porch to hold the platform level while working. You do not have to angle the porch joists as shown; we normally do for aesthetic reasons, but you may leave them square if desired, which is actually a little bit easier to build. If you choose to install a trapdoor, the easiest location is in line with the tree trunk, either on the porch or inside the house. Framing it in line with the tree will minimize the disruption of full-length floor joists.

## Stage 5

After all joists are installed, add knee braces, one at a time. First, check that your temporary bracing is holding the floor joists level. Then we suggest cutting a notch into the top of the knee brace to fit the platform frame. Next hold the knee brace up in place to mark the length of the bottom. Then bring the knee brace down to a work table, cut the length, and install the knee brace bracket into the wood. Last, hold the finished knee brace up in place, screw the top notch into the rim joists, mark the center of the hole on the tree through the bracket, predrill the hole, and turn the bolt into the tree right through the bracket. Repeat on the other knee brace. Depending on the length of the cantilever and width of the deck, you may need two or three knee braces. Two are shown, but if adding a third, it should go right in the center in line with the tree trunk.

(See the video on installing knee braces at TreehouseSupplies.com.)

## Stage 6

Install ⅝x6 pressure-treated decking or another exterior decking material of your choice. If desired, you may put a plywood subfloor down for the portion of the deck that will be enclosed instead of the deck boards. We recommend using 2½-inch decking screws with a torx head, such as the GRK R4 screws. Screws are a far better choice than nails for flooring. Be sure to leave a 1- to 3-inch gap around the tree for growth expansion. If you chose to install a trapdoor, cut out the flooring in that area.

## Stage 7

We suggest framing all the walls on the ground and lifting them into position with the help of a friend or hoist system. However, if you don't have a flat spot on the ground, and the platform is large enough, then it may prove easier to frame the wall lying flat up on your completed platform. Frame the window and door rough openings per the manufacturers' recommendations. Next, determine the pitch of the roof and the amount of overhang you want. Build your ridge and install it in place with temporary supports. Install the roof rafters.

## Stage 8

Install the wall and roof sheathing, as well as your roof felt. If your treehouse will not get a finished interior, then consider using two layers of roof sheathing so nails don't stick down and show from the underside. If the roof is high out of reach, then this may not matter to you.

**Pro Tip:** Where possible, let your wall sheathing extend down past your wall's bottom plate, and attach it to the side of your floor joists as shown. It will lock the treehouse to your platform, which will make it very rigid and prevent flexing or sagging in your floor joists.

## Stage 9

Install your windows, doors, choice of siding, roofing, trim, and railings.

## Stage 10

Install accessories such as swings, rope ladders, cargo climb nets, fireman's poles, zip lines, and anything else you have your heart set on.

# PLAN #2:
# ONE TREE, 10X10 SQUARE

## Stage 1

Install two TAB 3x9 bolts and pipe brackets at desired height in the tree for the top of the tribeam. Be sure to have your pipe bracket on the TAB before you turn it into the tree.

(See the video on installing TABs at Treehousesupplies.com.)

## Stage 2

Cut and install the first two joists. These can be doubled 2x8s or a single 3x8 timber on each side of the tree. Attach pipe bracket to joists with 4-inch RSS screws or galvanized lag bolts.

## Stage 3

Attach your rim joists. Temporary 2x4 posts on the corners will help hold everything level while you work. If needed, you can detach one of the doubled joists from stage 2, slide it left or right a bit, and reattach. It's worth the time to make sure you build the structure square (not a parallelogram) and that it is centered on the tree trunk.

## Stage 4

Next, cut and install the rest of the common joists. Last, fill in the short joists and headers in the big openings in line with the tree trunk. I suggest screwing the joists in place instead of nailing so that if they need to be shifted, they will be easier to modify. I advise leaving 3 to 6 inches of space between joists and the tree to minimize future maintenance as the tree grows. If you choose to install a trapdoor, the easiest location is in line with the tree trunk. Framing it in line with the tree will minimize the disruption of full-length floor joists.

## Stage 5

After all joists are installed, add knee braces, one at a time. First, check that your temporary bracing is holding the floor joists level. Then we suggest cutting a notch into the top of the knee brace to fit the platform frame. Next hold the knee brace up in place to mark the length of the bottom. Then bring the knee brace down to a work table, cut the length, and install the knee brace bracket into the wood. Last, hold the finished knee brace up in place, screw the top notch into the rim joists, mark the center of the hole on the tree through the bracket, predrill the hole, and turn the bolt into the tree right through the bracket. Repeat as you work around the tree, checking and rechecking level as you go.

(See the video on installing knee braces at Treehousesupplies.com.)

## Stage 6

Install ⅝x6 pressure-treated decking or another exterior decking material of your choice. If desired, you may put a plywood subfloor down for the portion of the deck that will be enclosed instead of the deck boards. We recommend using 2½-inch decking screws with a torx head, such as the GRK R4 screws. Screws are a far better choice than nails for flooring. Be sure to leave a 1- to 3-inch gap around the tree for growth expansion. If you

**Key Tip:** If you finish the knee braces and realize that one corner is too low, you can jack up that corner and slightly move the knee brace and top board in a little and reattach. The top board is bolted into the underside of the floor joists, and moving it in might mean that you have to cut a new one, but it's a lot easier than moving the knee brace.

chose to install a trapdoor, cut out the flooring in that area.

## Stage 7

We suggest framing all the walls on the ground and lifting them into position with the help of a friend or hoist system. However, if you don't have a flat spot on the ground, and the platform is large enough, then it may prove easier to frame the wall lying flat up on your completed platform. Frame the window and door rough openings per the manufacturers' recommendations. Next, determine the pitch of the roof and the amount of overhang you want. Build your ridge and install it in place with temporary supports. Install the roof rafters.

## Stage 8

Install the wall and roof sheathing, as well as your roof felt. If your treehouse will not get a finished interior, then consider using two layers of roof sheathing so nails don't stick down and show from the underside. If the roof is high out of reach, then this may not matter to you.

**Key Tip:** Where possible, let your wall sheathing extend down past your wall's bottom plate and attach it to the side of your floor joists as shown. It will lock the treehouse to your platform, which will make it very rigid and prevent flexing or sagging in your floor joists.

## Stage 9

Install your windows, doors, choice of siding, roofing, trim, and railings.

The swing set–style beam requires cutting a hole in the wall of the treehouse and resting it on the floor of the house. To cut this hole, start with a ¼-inch pilot hole from the inside of the treehouse just above the bottom plate in the framing. Then you can finish the cut from the outside with a jigsaw or a more intermediate skilled plunge cut with a circular saw.

## Stage 10

Install accessories such as swings, rope ladders, cargo climb nets, fireman's poles, zip lines, and anything else you have your heart set on.

# PLAN #3: ONE TREE ACCESSORY PLATFORM

## Stage 1

Install two TAB 3x9 bolts and pipe brackets at desired height in the tree for the top of the tribeam. Be sure to have your pipe bracket on the TAB before you turn it into the tree.

(See the video on installing TABs at Treehousesupplies.com.)

## Stage 2

Cut and install the first two joists. These can be doubled 2x8s or a single 3x8 timber on each side of the tree. Attach pipe bracket to joists with 4-inch RSS screws or galvanized lag bolts.

## Stage 3

Attach your rim joists. Temporary 2x4 posts on the corners will help hold everything level while you work. If needed, you can detach one of the doubled joists from stage 2, slide it left or right a bit, and reattach. It's worth the time to make sure you build the structure square (not a parallelogram) and that it is centered on the tree trunk.

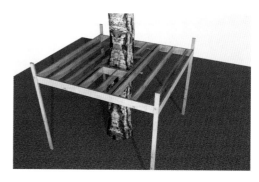

## Stage 4

Next, cut and install the rest of the common joists. Last, fill in the short joists and headers in the big openings in line with the tree trunk. I suggest screwing the joists in place instead of nailing so that if they need to be shifted, they will be easier to modify. I advise leaving 3 to 6 inches of space between joists and the tree to minimize future maintenance as the tree grows. If you choose to install a trapdoor, the easiest location is in line with the tree trunk. Framing it in line with the tree will minimize the disruption of full-length floor joists.

## Stage 5

After all joists are installed, add knee braces, one at a time. First, check that your temporary bracing is holding the floor joists level. Then we suggest cutting a notch into the top of the knee brace to fit the platform frame. Next, hold the knee brace up in place to mark the length of the bottom. Then bring the knee brace down to a work table, cut the length, and install the knee brace bracket into the wood. Last, hold the finished knee brace up in place, screw the top notch into the rim joists, mark the center of the hole on the tree through the bracket, predrill the hole, and turn the bolt into the tree right through the bracket. Repeat as you work around the tree, checking and rechecking level as you go.

(See the video on installing knee braces at Treehousesupplies.com.)

**Key Tip:** If you finish the knee braces and realize that one corner is too low, you can jack up that corner and slightly move the knee brace and top board in a little and reattach. The top board is bolted into the underside of the floor joists, and moving it in might mean that you have to cut a new one, but it's a lot easier than moving the knee brace.

## Stage 6

Install ⁵⁄₄x6 pressure-treated decking or another exterior decking material of your choice. If desired, you may put a plywood subfloor down for the portion of the deck that will be enclosed instead of the deck boards. We recommend using 2½-inch decking screws with a torx head, such as the GRK R4 screws. Screws are a far better choice than nails for flooring. Be sure to leave a 1- to 3-inch gap around the tree for growth expansion. If you chose to install a trapdoor, cut out the flooring in that area.

## Stage 7

Cut 4x4 posts at a work station on the ground, and then install them as desired. Normal post spacing is 3 to 6 inches apart, with 2x4 rails running horizontally. I always start by identifying which accessories and access points I want to have, because each of these requires a post on either side. In this case, we have a rope ladder, a cargo net, and a slide. The opening size for the rope ladder and slide should be approximately 24 to 30 inches wide. Tube slides sometimes require larger openings. The cargo net is always a custom order and can be made any width you like, but for a project like this, I would make the opening 4 feet wide. Once you have a post set on either side of the openings, you can add posts to the corners and anywhere else as needed for stability. Notice that one post is taller, which will allow a pulley and bucket to be attached later. After the posts are installed, the 2x4s are installed next. I like to leave the top 2x4 intact everywhere except where stairways are, which makes it safer. The bottom 2x4 should be cut where you have to sit down to exit, such as a slide or a fireman's pole.

## Stage 8

Install swing, rope ladder, cargo climb net, and slide. The swings can be tied around the beam with rope, but are more typically installed with pivoting swing hanger hardware.

The spider swing is shown here in a double-rope configuration, which makes it swing back and forth only, but all four ropes can be joined at one spot to make it go in any direction, like a tire swing would.

The swing set–style beam is best installed on top of the platform and bolted into a secure railing post. The other side of the A-frame should be built with each side either 25 or 30 degrees off plumb. The more the legs spread, the more vigorously you can swing without tipping the frame.

# PLAN #4:
# THREE TREES WITH BRIDGE

## Stage 1

Install TAB 3x9 bolt and pipe bracket at desired height in the tree for the top of the tribeam. Be sure to have your pipe bracket on the TAB before you turn it into the tree.

(See the video on installing TABs at Treehousesupplies.com.)

## Stage 2

Build the tribeam on the ground and then with help, lift and attach it to the pipe bracket located on the top TAB bolt. A rope-and-pulley system makes this easier to lift, especially when building out of easy reach. Once it is in place, hold the top part of the tribeam level, and then mark the location for the bottom TAB through the hole in the bracket at the bottom of the tribeam. Drill for the bottom TAB, but we suggest tilting the tribeam

and inserting the bottom TAB into the bracket before turning the TAB into the tree. We can usually put this TAB in the tree without disconnecting the tribeam from the upper TAB and bracket.

(See the video on building tribeams at Treehousesupplies .com.)

## Stage 3

Install TABs for beam. As shown with a 12-foot-wide treehouse, this beam should be an engineered

**Key Tip:** Before installing TABs, you should mark the location of all TABs on the main floor level. Don't worry about the crow's nest of the bottom of the tribeam just yet. Mark the centers of the TABs on each tree. Don't forget to adjust for various brackets and beam thicknesses. If one side has a pipe bracket and the other has a floating bracket, you will need to adjust the side with the floating bracket down by ½ inch to account for the extra thickness. This will become apparent when you have the hardware in hand to look at. Also, keep in mind that you might be using a taller beam on one side than on the other side, and TABs will need to be adjusted up or down in order to end up with a level floor. I find it extremely helpful to choose one TAB as a baseline and to double-check all measurements.

beam because the span between the TABs will end up being approximately 15 to 16 feet. I would use a 3.5x14–inch treated glulam or treated Parallam beam. There are various sizes available, so if your treehouse will be smaller or larger according to the spacing of your tree trunks, then you can adjust the size of the beam accordingly.

## Stage 4

Next, cut and install the rest of the common joists. I suggest screwing the joists in place instead of nailing so that if they need to be shifted, they will be easier to modify. I advise leaving 3 to 6 inches of space between joists and the tree to minimize future maintenance as the tree grows. If you choose to install a trapdoor, the easiest location is in line with the tree trunk. Framing it in line with the tree will minimize the disruption of full-length floor joists.

The hexagonal platform is similar to plan #2 in that it uses the same two TABs under the main floor and four knee braces at the perimeter for support. The formula for calculating the side length of hexagons is Diameter (flat to flat) divided by 1.732 equals Side Length. If you want a 10-foot-wide hexagon, take 120 inches, divide by 1.732, and get 69¼ inches for the length of each side. Your angles will be 30 and 60 degrees. As a side note, if you prefer octagons, then take 120, divide by 2.414, and get 49¾ inches for the length of the side, and your angles will be 22.5 and 45 degrees.

The crow's nest is best installed by an experienced tree climber. The two ⁵⁄₄x15–inch galvanized lag bolts with pipe brackets are installed first. Next, all of the joists should be cut and assembled on the ground. With a block and tackle of either 3:1 or 5:1, hoist the joists up into position and connect the pipe brackets to the frame.

Last, install the knee braces before disconnecting the hoist system.

(See the video on installing knee braces at Treehousesupplies.com.)

## Stage 5

Install ⁵⁄₄x6 pressure-treated decking or another exterior decking material of your choice. If desired, you may put a plywood subfloor down for the portion of the deck that will be enclosed instead of the deck boards. We recommend using 2½-inch decking screws with a torx head, such as the GRK R4 screws. Screws are a far better choice than nails for flooring. Be sure to leave a 1- to 3-inch gap around the tree for growth expansion. If you chose to install a trapdoor, cut out the flooring in that area.

## Stage 6

We suggest framing all the walls on the ground and lifting them into position with the help of a friend or hoist system. However, if you don't have a flat spot on the ground, and the platform is large enough, then it may prove easier to frame the wall lying flat up on your completed platform. Frame the window and door rough openings per the manufacturers' recommendations. Next, determine the pitch of the roof and the amount of overhang you want. Build your ridge and install it in place with temporary supports. Install the roof rafters.

## Stage 7

Install the wall and roof sheathing, as well as your roof felt. If your treehouse will not get a finished interior, then consider using two layers of roof sheathing so nails don't stick down and show from the underside. If the roof is high out of reach, then this may not matter to you.

**Key Tip:** Where possible, let your wall sheathing extend down past your wall's bottom plate and attach it to the side of your floor joists as shown. It will lock the treehouse to your platform, which will make it very rigid and prevent flexing or sagging in your floor joists.

## Stage 8

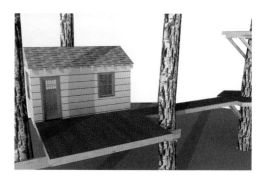

Install your windows, doors, choice of siding, roofing, and trim. Bridges can be of two basic types: rigid or flexible. The rigid bridges will need structural members such as beams and joists. The flexible ones will sag and be supported by wires in tension. Our store sells kits with rope, netting, metal connectors, and large eyebolts for the flexible bridge types. The kits come with detailed instructions. If you prefer a rigid bridge, then you can use conventional lumber to connect both platforms. For rigid bridges, be sure to allow a small amount of flexibility for when the trees sway independently. One side should have a sliding plate, hanging beam, or other connection type that will not fail in windy weather.

## Stage 9

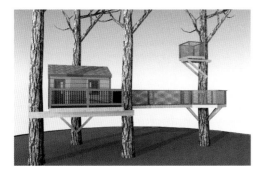

This project uses some black aluminum spindles on the main treehouse and netting railings everywhere else. Netting is flexible and so is the best choice for flexible bridge styles. We connect netting either with border ropes and knots or with a pneumatic stapler that shoots 1-inch crown staples. The aluminum spindles are a more polished look and feel, and each brand has specific connectors to use and instructions to follow.

Normally you would install 4x4 posts first, then 2x4 horizontal railings, and then railing fill. However, for the section with the aluminum spindles, you may need to install the 2x4s and the spindles simultaneously.

## Stage 10

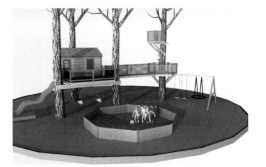

Install accessories such as swings, rope ladders, cargo climb nets, fireman's poles, zip lines, and anything else you have your heart set on.

The GAGA pit shown here is a game that keeps groups of kids running around for hours. The full rules are available online, but in short, they run around hitting the ball into each other's feet and lower legs to put each other out, and the last kid in is the winner. We designed a kit with the green brackets shown, which is for sale with instructions on our website. The brackets can be used for an octagon of any size, and the octagon size formula may be used to calculate side length: Diameter (flat to flat) divided by 2.414 equals side length. My favorite size is the

20-foot GAGA pit. Start with 240-inch diameter, divide by 2.414, get sides that are 99⅜ inches long. An 8-foot board is 96 inches, so I hate to buy a 10-foot board just for an extra 3⅜ Inches. Call me cheap, but I hate waste. I would make the sides at 96 inches, and have a pit that is 19 feet 3¾ inches to save a few bucks and not waste lumber.

Either way, kids have a ball for hours with this game.

Another unique accessory shown here are the two hanging swings under the main treehouse. This style of hammock swing is made by many manufacturers. Some have cup holders and foot rests built in. They hang from a single rope and are a great place for a nap.

# PLAN #5: FOUR TREES

**Stage 1**

Install TAB 6x12 bolts and floating brackets at desired height in the tree. Be sure to have your brackets on the TABs before you turn them into the trees.

(See the video on installing TABs at Treehousesupplies.com.)

## Stage 2

Add the TABs for the second beam. As an alternative, you can substitute one of the floating brackets for a pipe bracket, which will make that tree a master, and the other three trees will float within their slots.

## Stage 3

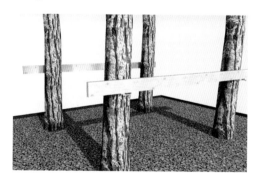

As shown, these beams should be engineered beams because the span between the TABs will end up approximately 14 feet, and the load in the center will be high. I would use a 3.5x14–inch treated

**Key Tip:** For a large treehouse like this, which is 20x20 feet as shown, you should always use the largest standard TABs we offer, which are the 6x12s. They will support substantially more load than the smaller ones. If you need help deciding, please contact us before ordering.

glulam or treated Parallam beam. There are various sizes available, so if your treehouse will be smaller or larger according to the spacing of your tree trunks, then you can adjust the size of the beam accordingly.

## Stage 4

Next, cut and install the floor joists. I suggest screwing the joists in place instead of nailing so that if they need to be shifted, they will be easier to modify. I advise leaving 3 to 6 inches of space between joists and the tree to minimize future maintenance as the tree grows. If you choose to install a trapdoor, the easiest location is in line with the tree trunk. Framing it in line with the tree will minimize the disruption of full-length floor joists.

These floor joists span approximately 16 feet, which means that they should be 2x12. Additionally, you should install extra joists underneath the house to help transfer the house loads outward toward the beams.

## Stage 5

Install ⁵⁄₄x6 pressure-treated decking or another exterior decking material of your choice. If desired, you may put a plywood subfloor down for the portion of the deck that will be enclosed instead of the deck boards. We recommend using 2½-inch decking screws with a torx head, such as the GRK R4 screws. Screws are a far better choice than nails for flooring. Be sure to leave a 1- to 3-inch gap around the tree for growth expansion. If you chose to install a trapdoor, cut out the flooring in that area.

## Stage 6

Normally I suggest framing all the walls on the ground and lifting them into position with the help of a friend or hoist system. However, with the size of this platform, the best place to frame the walls is right on the platform. Frame the window and door rough openings per the manufacturers' recommendations. Next, determine the pitch of the roof and the amount of overhang you want. Build your ridge and install it in place with temporary supports. Install the roof rafters.

## Stage 7

Install the wall and roof sheathing, as well as your roof felt. If your treehouse will not get a finished interior, then consider using two layers of roof sheathing so nails don't stick down and show from the underside. If the roof is high out of reach, then this may not matter to you. If you are not going to heat or air-condition the treehouse, then you might skip the wall sheathing and simply install the siding directly onto the wall frame.

## Stage 8

This siding is T 1-11 plywood, which is graded for exterior exposure. I strongly suggest staining it for looks and better weathering. It can be installed with minimum 2-inch screws or with ring shank nails.

Irregular cedar shakes are shown here on the roof, which can be installed over plywood or lath.

## Stage 9

Install windows and doors and exterior trim on the building. Trim can be treated wood, cedar, or any material you have left over.

Be creative and resourceful. The point of trim is just to cover the cut edges of siding material and the flanges from new construction windows.

Cut 4x4 posts at a work station on the ground, and then install them as desired. Normal post spacing is 3 to 6 inches apart, with 2x4 rails running horizontally. Normally you would install 4x4 posts first, then 2x4 horizontal railings, and then railing fill. However, when using metal spindles as shown, you may need to install the 2x4s and the spindles simultaneously per the instructions that come with the spindles. Alternatively, you can use cedar or pressure-treated 2x2 spindles, which are screwed on after the 2x4 rails are installed.

## Stage 10

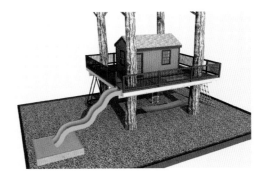

Install accessories such as swings, rope ladders, cargo climb nets, fireman's poles, zip lines, and anything else you have your heart set on.

Large platforms like this are great for monkey bars, swings, and hammocks underneath. Just make sure that the accessories are spaced far enough apart that kids don't crash into each other while swinging.

# CHAPTER 6

# CONSTRUCTION TIPS NOTEBOOK

## WORKING AT HEIGHT

To date, and I hope forever, our company has not had a serious climbing injury due to falling. Proper climbing techniques, regular equipment inspection, patience, and good judgment have kept us on the right path. However, we have had tools and materials dropped on people, bee stings, ant swarms, ladder shifts, and some near misses.

When working over 6 feet high, it is very good practice to observe the following:

1. Secure all ladders to the tree or platform.
2. Remain tied in to your safety rope while at height.
3. Wear a helmet.

Always secure tools that you take aloft to make climbing safer and easier.

4. Declare a danger zone where nobody on the ground stands while others are aloft.
5. Secure all tools and materials that you take with you.

For additional information about climbing techniques, please refer to the Help and Resources section.

## RIGGING

The term "rigging" harkens back to the early system of ropes and pulleys used to hoist the sails on a ship up to the top of the mast. There were at

Left: Lifting large beams is done easily with the right equipment. Right: This section of turning stair tread was easier to build on the ground and then hoist into position.

least two strong benefits for using pulleys. The first was redirection. No sailors had to climb to the top of the mast and pull upward. Instead they could keep a pulley set at the top and pull downward from the deck. This saved time and increased safety. The second benefit was the mechanical advantage gained by setting multiple pulleys, which reduced the amount of pulling force required to lift the sail.

In treehouse building, while we aren't usually lifting sails, rigging systems are sometimes necessary for heavy lifting and working very high in the air. Rigging can save a lot of time and effort by allowing you to lift heavy beams or sections of walls from a safe position on the ground. However, if your treehouse is only going to be 6 feet high and relatively small, then you can probably get by with conventional lifting methods. We generally set up rigging to lift long support poles and set them into the ground, lift large beams that sometimes weigh around 1,000 pounds, lift single tree platform frames up to set them on the TABs, and lift wall sections up one at a time. There are plenty of other circumstances where rigging is useful, but those are the common ones. One project required that we set up a rigging line to transport all of our building materials and tools down a cliff, and hoist tools and trash back up at the end.

## MATH MINUTE

Mechanical advantage is the reduction ratio from the load being lifted to the force you apply to lift it. Remember the block and tackle diagrams from physics class? They were confusing to me back then too. But the simple way to think about it is to count how many ropes you are pulling on (this should be one!), and how many ropes are getting shorter. If three ropes are getting shorter, then you have a 3:1 mechanical advantage. Friction does reduce the efficiency, so using a real block and tackle with a large sheave instead of a loop in the rope or a small cheap pulley will reduce your friction dramatically. The most common systems we use for lifting are 1:1, 3:1, and 5:1.

## Rigging Poles

First, dig the hole. Then set the pole bottom halfway into the hole and place a vertical board in the back of the hole to stop the pole from sliding too far. Then set the main block and tackle to lift the top of the pole over the hole. Start lifting. Once the pole leaves the ground, it will have a tendency to swing side-to-side. To counteract this, affix a tag line heading 90 degrees to the block and tackle in both directions. A tag line is a spare rope to guide an object into position as it is being lifted. Then finish lifting, with one or two people lifting the main line and one person holding a tag line on each side of the pole for stabilization. We have lifted utility poles 30 feet long with this method. It is easier if you have a high-angle tree branch to set the block and tackle line on, which greatly reduces the force needed to lift.

## Rigging Beams

The first step is to install the TABs on both trees. With two block and tackle systems, set one on each side of the two trees and lift evenly. Using two block and tackle systems is easier, but it can be done with only one if necessary. Here are two ways to accomplish this with one block and tackle.

If you can lift the center of the beam and control the rotation with tag lines, then that is optimal. You may need to set the top block high in one tree and redirect the block closer to the center with another line. Alternatively, if you can't lift the center, then set the block and tackle as close to the center as possible, and set a 1:1 system on the other side as close to the end as possible. This method will work, but the 1:1 side will be harder to lift. Another tactic is to hoist one side, secure it, and then move the block and tackle to lift the other side.

Controlling the block location by adjusting the direction of pull is a trick that experience will teach you. If you set the top pulley very close to the tree, then it won't sway much as you pull. However, if you experiment using

Rigging beams

a longer sling so that the pulley can move about 4 feet to 8 feet from the tie point, then you will determine the final position of the pulley by the direction you pull the down line from. With practice you can then pull the lifting line in the direction where you want the top block to move to while lifting. With this method you can lift more precisely. You can also allow a beam to rise a few feet away from the trunk, and then walk toward the tree to let the beam settle back toward the trunk and rest on a TAB, which protects the tree bark while lifting. You will impress people doing this all by yourself from the ground. You can similarly adjust a beam side by side by walking to new pull positions while lifting.

## Rigging Single Tree Platforms

I used to assemble platforms in the air one board at a time. It is completely doable if you don't mind spending a lot of time in a climbing harness and working in awkward positions that require a lot of core strength. However, I found that the fastest way to build a single tree platform is to completely cut each joist and assemble them all at the cut site. Then, loosen enough screws to carry the platform to the tree in two pieces. The two pieces can be set on 2- to 3-foot-tall temporary stilts that can be made of scrap wood. The two halves should then be reassembled around the base of the tree about 2 to 3 feet off the ground. If the tree tapers significantly, then you may have to remove one of the center joists in order to connect the two halves; this is fine, because one joist will be enough to rest the platform on one of the two TABs.

To rig for lifting, we set a block and tackle up on one side of the tree and set lifting slings so that the block and tackle will be lifting about two-thirds to three-fourths of the weight of the platform. On the opposite side of the tree, we set a single line with only one pulley for redirection. This line is only lifting one-fourth to one-third of the load, and is used to control tilt. In this configuration, one worker on each line is usually sufficient to hoist an 8- to 12-foot platform as high as you want. One last step before liftoff:

Lifting platform joists as one, using a 5:1 system and 1:1 balancing line

Tie a tag line onto the edge of the platform, which will be used to rotate the platform 90 degrees to allow the floor to clear the two TABs (already installed opposite each other in the tree). After the 90-degree turn, lift the platform over the TABs, release the tag line, and then the platform will rotate back to the correct orientation on the TABs and you can lower the platform onto the TABs. Once set onto one of the TABs, ropes are secured and a climber ascends to connect the platform frame to the brackets and start filling in any pieces of joists that had to be removed for lifting. Leave the rigging ropes in place until all knee braces are installed so that they can help in leveling the platform during installation. Once the knee braces are in place, you can use the rigging lines to lift the floor boards up to the deck.

# SHOE DAISY TREEHOUSE

Working on siding and roofing high in the air requires a lot of time spent either waiting on a ground helper or climbing up and down. As we built the Shoe Daisy Treehouse at Treehouse World, we opted to frame, side, and shingle the roof on the deck, and then hoist the entire roof up with dual 5:1 hoist systems. We then built the curved walls underneath them, and then set the roof down on top! The tree-collar flashing and windows were set in place afterward. The Shoe Daisy Treehouse is themed on the Mother Goose poem about the old woman who lived in a shoe.

We framed the Shoe Daisy Treehouse from the top down to limit climbing time.

## Rigging Walls

It's a really cute trick to build walls on the ground, sheath them, side them, and then hoist them up into place—windows, trim, and all. If you are going to attempt it, then please remember to measure twice. Do not forget to account for the lean of the tree trunk, or you might build the house too big for the space between two trees. The walls may be several hundred pounds if they include windows and siding, so you should ensure that you can set the block in a good location to lift the wall directly outside one edge of the platform. The edge of the platform is the easiest location for someone to handle the wall and orient it properly. Nothing is worse than realizing that you can't get the wall hoisted and have to take it apart and go about it the traditional way.

Given the pros and cons of wall hoisting, we don't do it often. Hoisting walls makes the most sense when the platform is not big enough to build the wall laid out on the treehouse deck and stand it up in place, or when the platform is higher than about 20 feet. In the latter case, it's better to hoist because it becomes time-consuming to work from ladders and ropes. For projects under 15 feet tall, you can hand most materials from the ground up to a nice flat platform and build the walls in place. Another consideration is travel. If you want to shorten the time that you are on the building site, you can build wall and roof sections in a shop and truck them to the site. We occasionally do this for projects that are far away or when we want to get work accomplished inside on a rainy or snowy day.

## LIFTING TECHNIQUE: SCISSOR JACK

There are countless situations during treehouse building when you need to lift something heavy a short distance and hold it still. For example, if the joists are in the air, you definitely want to lift and hold the platform level while installing a single knee brace to the perimeter. Actually, I prefer to hold the platform about ¼ inch high because of inevitable compression at the tree end of the knee brace, but the point is the same. You can lift from above with block and tackle, but the scissor jack technique is perfect for this.

Set a block on the ground if desired to prevent the jack from settling into the dirt (not shown). Attach a 2x4 into the rim joist with a single RSS screw or other large fastener. Attach a second 2x4 to the first one as shown. Then push both 2x4s into alignment to lift the joist or beam. Check level and, if necessary, release the jack and adjust the angle between the two 2x4s and lift again. It may take a few iterations to get the correct amount of lift, but

Left to right: Attach 2x4s together with RSS screw or single bolt. Push 2x4s to line them up, which lifts the beam or joist. Tack a second screw through both 2x4s to keep them from springing back while you work.

you will be surprised how easy this is to lift several hundred pounds and hold it still. This one tip may prove worth the price of this book.

## OUTDOOR-STYLE FLOORING

Perhaps the simplest flooring option that will last is to use an outdoor decking such as ⅝x6 lumber. This is commonly available across the United States in pressure-treated pine, cedar, and composite. There are other special-order materials such as tropical hardwood, which is a rare species with low production.

Most decks are built by spacing joists out at 16 inches on center and laying ⅝x6 boards perpendicular to the joists. The boards need two screws per board at each joist. Screws are much better than nails for this purpose, because nails can loosen up over time. Some composite boards come with blind fastening clips, which keep screw heads out of the surface of the decking. This practice provides a cleaner look when finished. Of course, you

|                         | Pressure Treated | Cedar    | Composite | Tropical Hardwood |
|-------------------------|------------------|----------|-----------|-------------------|
| Cost                    | $                | $$       | $$$       | $$$               |
| Longevity               | Moderate         | Moderate | Excellent | Excellent         |
| Maintenance Required    | Moderate         | High     | Low       | Moderate          |

can use other dimensions of wood for flooring, but wide boards don't drain as well, so they aren't the longest-lasting choice for outdoor surfaces.

**Waterproofing Tip:** Water can creep under the sill plate of the house if you just set the wall on top of the decking. The water lands outside on the deck and runs along the top of the decking board underneath the wall plate. The best way to stop that is to add a couple extra joists at the edges of exterior walls and create a break in the decking large enough for flashing to divert

A solid interior subfloor is ¾ inch thick and moisture resistant.

Start by installing the interior subfloor, leave a gap for drainage, and run exterior deck boards around the plywood.

water below the flooring. A simpler method is to silicone caulk the outside of the bottom plate, but this may not last as long as flashing that extends below the flooring. On simple kids' treehouses where a bit of moisture isn't a problem, you can skip this step to save time and money.

The interior of the treehouse can be anything you like. Indoor/Outdoor spaces should stick to outdoor-style decking for drainage, and they can be covered with outdoor carpet for some color and more playful appearance. Using ¾-inch plywood sheathing is a good idea, as it is very strong. If you're going for a one-layer floor, then pick a sanded plywood with a smooth appearance and stain both sides. The bottom side at least should be stained on the ground and dried before installation. You can choose a CDX plywood to save about 50–60 percent of the plywood cost—it is just as strong but doesn't have a smooth veneer layer. OSB is the cheapest plywood, but I would avoid using regular OSB on a floor; the moisture-ready variety is OK, but the cost difference is not significant enough for me to recommend that option.

The best floors have a sheathing layer and a finish layer just like in a ground house. For the subfloor, if it's getting covered up, you can find pressure-treated plywood, but it's not usually a stock item. We normally use the most weather-resistant ¾-inch plywood available, such as what would go in a bathroom or basement over concrete, which normally comes in 4x8 tongue-and-groove sheets. If you are only putting one layer of plywood down for the floor and you're in a dry area, then you can use a finished plywood, which is smoother and looks a lot nicer. If you use this material, don't forget to stain the bottom side before installing for some protection. Finished plywood often has problems if it gets wet. Then the finish floor goes on top. It can be old barn boards, brand-new hardwood floors, carpet, tile, or anything that makes the place yours. Don't forget stain, throw rugs, and a welcome mat outside the door!

## STAIRS AND LADDERS

Stairs and ladders are the primary ways to access a treehouse. Ladders are steeper, simpler, cheaper, and normally have 2x4 or 2x6 stringers, and they take up less space. Stairs are built to code with typical rules regarding the rise and run, generally have 2x12 stringers, take longer to build, and take up more space. If the entrance is a trapdoor, then ladders are preferred, because code stairs require a very large opening overhead, which often uses too much interior floor space.

## Ladders

I am not aware of codes for ladder building, but I can tell you how we build them based on customer feedback over the years. You want the rise of each step to be somewhere between 9 and 12 inches for most kids to easily

Pull down on the log to open the trapdoor before climbing!

Trapdoors are extremely popular with kids. By using a counterweight log or a piston hinge, you can make the door easier to open. A sturdy rim around the inside of the opening will make the door safer to walk on when it is closed. I recommend using lightweight lumber such as red cedar for the door material.

The piston hinge slows the closing of the trapdoor and makes it easier to open.

climb. If you build a ladder according to common stairway code (with rises of 7¾ inches), then it will not feel right at all to climb.

The best angle for climbing the ladder is about 25 degrees from plumb. Of course, if space is the only important factor, then you can build it straight up and down. Twenty to 25 degrees works well with 2x6 stringers and 2x6 treads, but if you build the ladder at 30 degrees or more, you will wish it had 2x8 treads to feel safer.

Ladder width should be approximately 25 inches, which means inset treads will be at 22 inches. Attaching the steps can be done simply by using three or more screws of at least 3 inches in length from each side, screwing right through the stringer into the end grain of the tread. Make sure the screws hit the middle or lower part of the tread so that the tread doesn't split out. Since all wood gets weaker over time, an extra step to build stronger tread attachments is to put a metal angle bracket or a block of wood under each end of the treads and fasten it to the stringer. This will make the tread significantly stronger and longer lasting.

The simplest of ladders is to lean up a couple 2x4 stringers and then cut 2x4 treads and screw them to the top surface of the stringers. No notching, no insetting, no blocking. I use this method only on an interior ladder up to a loft because it is very compact and lightweight. Remember not to leave spaces between 4 and 9 inches between the steps, because doing so could lead to entrapment.

## Stairs

The goal of the stair builder is for each rise and run to be the same all the way up the stairs so people don't accidentally trip. (Many medieval castle designers intentionally built stairs with changing rises and runs to confuse invaders and make them stumble.) Carefully measure the elevation change from the treehouse down to the ground. Make sure to account for the slope of the ground in the direction that stairs will be built. You can usually level from the top over with a long 2x4 or a string line and line level.

## Example for Stair Stringer Layout

a.  Calculate number of steps: Divide the total elevation change of 96 inches by 7.75 inches. Answer is 12.39. Round up to 13 steps, because rounding down will lead to rises over 7.75 inches.

b.  Calculate rise of each step: 96 inches / 13 steps = 7.38 inches per step.

c.  Determine run per step: The minimum depth of each step for IRC compliance is 10 inches; however, then you must use a ¾-inch to ⅝-inch overhang. If you prefer to avoid that, then choose 11 inches for the run. I generally choose 11 inches.

d.  Lay out the stringer: If the board has a crown, face that up on the side of the board where treads will be (the pointy side). Use a framing square to mark each rise and run.

e.  Remove the tread thickness from the bottom step. You need to do this because when you add the treads, your first step would be 7.38 inches + 1 inch = 8.38 inches for the first step. So you should mark and cut the 1 inch off now. Of course, if your treads are 2x6 instead of ⅝x6, then remove 1.5 inches instead.

f.  Adjust for site-specific conditions. If you are going to set the bottom of the stringers on a stone or board that will be set aboveground and be flush with the end of the stairs, then you should also remove the thickness of that material from the bottom step.

g.  Use this pattern to trace more stringers. Most 3-foot-wide staircases are built with three to four stringers. I usually prefer four stringers for staircases that are over about 6 feet tall. This is just my personal preference for making sure that the stairs don't feel bouncy in the middle.

h.  Attach the stringers. I have two favorite ways to do this:

1. Directly connect the back of the stringer to a rim joist of the treehouse. I like to use 90-degree-angled brackets and/or screw from the inside of the rim joist with 6-inch timber screws.

2. Hang each stringer from the rim joist with approximately 18-inch metal strap ties or custom steel straps, secured with joist hanger nails and some 3-inch or 4-inch timber screws to ensure nails don't loosen up from tree movement.

## Dealing with Tree Movement at the Stairs

If a staircase is rigidly attached at the top and bottom, then a small amount of tree movement, even ½ to 1 inch, can cause one of the two connections to break. The longer the staircase, the more movement will occur between the top to bottom of the stairs. Most breaks I have seen are at 6-foot elevation change or longer stairs, but anything is possible. At 12-foot change or greater, it's almost guaranteed to be a problem. The way to deal with it is to allow one end of the stairs to float.

### Bottom Floating Stairs

I usually prefer to let the bottom float while securely attaching the tops of the steps. This can be done by building a small ramp under the stringers that the stairs can slide upward on a couple inches and slide back down when the wind switches direction to reset the stairs in exactly the same spot. We also build a track to limit the sideways travel of the stairs, which can be done on the inside to hide the unusual-looking framing.

**Pro Tip:** Line the ramp and landing plate with UHMW plastic or some other low-friction sliding plate. This device will allow small

## WHY BUILD A RAMP?

When long ladders are set on the ground and rigidly attached at the top, wind can seriously damage the treehouse. When the wind blows away from the stairs, it drags the stairs inward. Then when the wind blows back toward the stairs, the bottoms of the stringers can dig in, which after several iterations can jack up the edge of a platform. That is why we build ramps to reset the stairs in the same place.

movement and reset your stairs every time.

### Top Floating Stairs

If the bottom of the stairs or ladder will be permanently mounted, then there are a couple ways to allow the top to float. I have experimented with these but do not use them often. The first is to double up your outer stair stringers; use a thicker tread that can span the 36-inch width, and let both stringers rest on top of the deck and stick several inches past the edge of the deck over the inside of the platform. The stringers will slide on the deck or rim joist when the wind blows. Either

The Pirate Ship Treehouse at Treehouse World has a top floating staircase on the way up to the crow's nest. The crow's nest is 15 feet higher than the main deck, which means that the lateral movement regularly exceeds an inch. The bottom of the ladder is bolted down, and the top slides on a low-friction UHMW plate. The Pirate Ship Treehouse includes a one-of-a-kind activity called Walk the Plank. There are three planks between 20 and 35 feet high where you must wear a harness and take a leap of faith. I built it, so trust me when I say that it's scarier than it sounds.

The top floating stairs allow the tree to sway over a 16-foot distance between decks.

notch a groove in the floor to trap the stringers side to side, or locate railing posts or other wood to limit side-to-side movement. Again, a pro tip is to line the underside of the stringer and/or the rub points on the deck with UHMW to prevent squeaking and wood damage due to rubbing. A second way to do this is to suspend the stringers from a cable or chain that can allow an appropriate amount of tree movement, but this is more difficult to do safely.

## WALLS

I have built many styles of walls over the years based on the design style and purpose of the treehouse. Most kids' treehouses can have 2x3 or 2x4 construction with just one layer of siding directly affixed to the studs. You can then appreciate the character of your finished siding from the inside and outside of the treehouse. This is not the most weatherproof method, as there is only one layer and there may be knots or cracks in the boards,

Siding and roofing applied directly to framing in one layer

Four-season climate-controlled treehouses need insulation and weatherproofing layers.

Don't forget color! It adds a lot of character to your project and helps protect wood from weathering elements. If using T 1-11 or other plywood siding, then apply a semitransparent or solid color stain to the exterior. To minimize ladder time, consider staining before you install the material. Don't forget about the inside—if the inside of the siding will show between the studs, then consider staining the inside of the siding first so that you don't have to do any cutting in. It also allows for easily painting the studs a different color if desired.

A castle can have two color themes. Use solid color stain for this look.

This transparent stain darkens and protects the siding but doesn't hide the wood grain.

but it is faster, lighter, less expensive, and yet is still weatherproof enough for a treehouse that is not going to be climate controlled. However, if you are adding a heater or air conditioner and don't want the treehouse to be drafty, then going through the added steps of sheathing the outside of the wall, adding a vapor/moisture barrier, and then installing finish siding will be the best way to go. For permanent homes, we also add insulation and interior wall finishing.

Walls serve several structural purposes. The first is transferring dead load and snow load from the roof into the floor. This is achieved by placing wall

## WALL ASSEMBLY— NAILS OR SCREWS?

Walls in ground houses are always nailed together as opposed to screws. Nail guns make the process so much faster. When building a treehouse there are three reasons why I often screw the walls together instead: 1) Nails sometimes loosen up when you hoist a wall up to a platform. 2) In the event that overlapping siding is not an option, screws help keep the wall and roof tied down to the floor frame. 3) Sometimes, for smaller treehouses, the minimal time savings isn't worth bringing an air compressor, hoses, and nail guns with me to the work site.

studs on regular intervals (often 16 inches on center in conventional construction) and then building the roof with a rafter setting on the wall plate directly above each stud. Walls also lock the floor to the roof, which provides shear strength and tensile strength to resist wind forces, including uplift. You can use rafter ties to hold the roof down and strap ties to hold the wall down to the floor. As an alternative, you can use timber screws up through the top plate into the rafters, and also down through the bottom plate into the floor joists. Lastly, and at the risk of stating the obvious, walls serve a structural function of keeping people from falling out if they lean between studs. All sheathing and siding should be attached with screws or ring shanked nails, which resist loosening. As a safety test for the strength of the wall, you should be able to kick moderately hard between the studs and not loosen any of the siding.

## WINDOW TIPS AND TRICKS

There are several options for windows that work well in treehouses that would almost never appear in a ground house. For higher-end treehouses that our clients will be heating or air-conditioning, we generally go to a well-known window company, pay regular ground house prices, and wait four to eight weeks for our custom orders. When energy efficiency is not as important as budget, we use and resell single-hung windows that are single-pane tempered glass with screens and come with white or brown

Plexiglass covering a shape or design can make your own window light.

Silicone caulk on the outside helps seal this custom opening in the door.

aluminum cladding. You can also be creative by making your own windows and custom cutouts for art and light.

## CUTTING RAFTERS

There are several ways to cut rafters, but it helps to understand that they are all based on grade school math. You basically need to dig deep and remember $A^2 + B^2 = C^2$, how to multiply fractions, and then think through what you are doing. All of the required calculations can be completed on the calculator on a cell phone, with advanced functions such as squares and soh-cah-toa functions. Of all the methods out there, here is the way that I have always gone from wall measurements to rafter lengths:

*Example #1*
Givens: Gable roof style, 8/12 pitch, 10x10 treehouse

Every rafter length calculation starts with identifying a right triangle. I like to start with the inside corner of the wall at point X and move to beneath the near side of the ridge at point Y, and rise up to the near lower corner of the ridge at point Z.

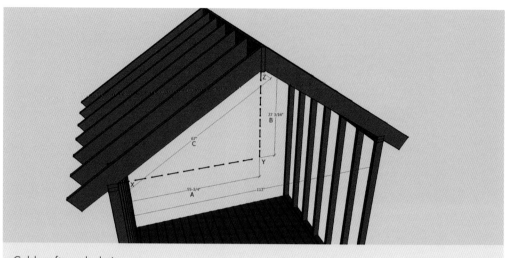

Gable rafter calculation

a. The inside-to-inside measurement between the walls should be 113 inches if you use 2x4 walls (120 inches – 3.5 inches – 3.5 inches = 113 inches). A 10-foot treehouse has a total framing width of 120 inches. Each 2x4 wall is 3.5 inches thick.

b. Don't forget to subtract the thickness of the ridge. 113 inches – 1.5 inches = 111.5 inches.

c. Divide by 2. 111.5 inches / 2 = 55.75 inches. This is length A.

d. Roof pitch is given by the designer. In this case, it is 8/12 pitch, which means 8 inches of rise over 12 inches of run. This ratio will help us figure length B, once we have length A from the previous step. 55.75 inches x (8/12) = 37.17 inches. This is length B.

e. Now, since $A^2 + B^2 = C^2$, $(55.75^2) + (37.1^2) = C^2$.

f. $3{,}108 + 1{,}382 = C^2$.

g. $4{,}490 = C^2$. To easily take the square of 4,490, you can hit the $X^Y$ button, then tap .5, then tap =.

h. $67 = C$. Length C is 67 inches.

i. Now you can start cutting the rafter. Crown all rafters up for a more consistent roof, if desired. Use a small square to mark and cut the plumb cut of your rafter, which will meet the ridge at the top. The plumb cut for 8/12 pitch is 34 degrees—this should be marked on your square.

j.  Next, measure down the bottom side of the rafter 67 inches and make a mark.

k.  Use your square to make the seat cut to fit the thickness of the wall plus sheathing.

l.  Add a rafter tail as desired. Tails can be made to hold a fascia, soffit, or any given decorative pattern desired.

## Example #2

Givens: Shed Roof, 4/12 pitch, 8x8 treehouse, 6-foot-high lower wall

The right triangle for a shed roof is a little easier to identify visually. Sometimes you may know what wall heights are ahead of time, but not know the pitch of the roof. If you know both wall heights, you can divide the rise over the run and convert to a pitch expressed as X/12. You can then read the angle for that pitch from your square. However, in this example we are given the pitch and need to figure the difference in wall height and rafter length.

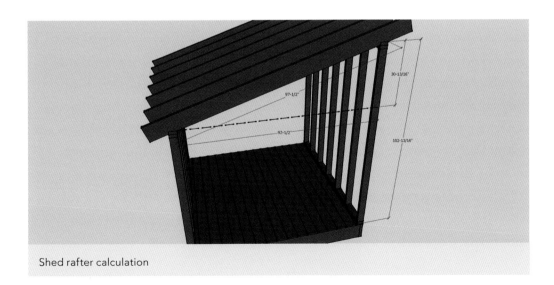

Shed rafter calculation

a.  With a 72-inch wall height on the low side, first we must calculate the height of the tall wall at 4/12 pitch. First, we calculate the run. The inside-to-outside measurement of the framing should be 92.5 inches with 2x4 walls (96 − 3.5 = 92.5). 92.5 inches is length A, or the run.

b.  Calculate rise. 92.5 inches x (4/12) = 30.83 inches, or $30\frac{13}{16}$. This is length B, or the rise.

c.  Top wall height is 72 inches + $30\frac{13}{16}$ = $102\frac{13}{16}$ inches. Now you can build the wall and then measure your rafter length. Or you can calculate and precut the rafters by following on.

d.  Now, since $A^2 + B^2 = C^2$, $(92.5^2) + (30.83^2) = C^2$.

e.  $8,556 + 950 = C^2$.

f.  $9,506 = C^2$. To easily take the square of 9,506, you can hit the $X^Y$ button, then tap .5, then tap =.

g.  97.5 = C. Length C is 97.5 inches.

h.  Now you can lay out and cut the rafter. The biggest mistake is not starting and finishing the rafter layout from the correct spots that are exactly in line with the pitch of the roof. On this roof the pitch starts at the inside of the lower wall frame and ends at the outside of the upper wall frame.

## ROOFING

You can use any roofing material on a treehouse that you would use on a ground house.However, the two that I recommend most often are metal panels and cedar shakes. I love the rustic look of shakes over lath, but they aren't especially durable and are above average in price. Metal is the economic choice: It is low cost, very durable, and comes in twenty different colors that are powder coated on. Another choice I like is the recycled shingles designed to look like slate. You can shoot them down with a standard roofing nailer, and they install easily, look nice, and are durable when installed over plywood. However, they are more expensive than cedar. There are many, many other choices that work well.

Metal roofing (white underside, color choices on top) over lath on hip roof frame

The roof functions to shed water, enclose a space, and look good. Any of the basic roof designs will shed water, but you may want to consider which direction the water will drip off the roof. Most people don't like water falling right in front of an exterior door, so you may want to choose a roof layout that diverts water away from the entry. To some, enclosing the space might mean just keeping birds and squirrels out, which might make a screened pergola a good simple choice, while to others that might mean keeping the heat inside. A low-pitch shed roof is the

Smoke-tinted polycarbonate roofing over lath on gazebo roof frame

Some roof styles make better loft spaces. Old barns often used gambrel roofs to allow more usable space in the loft than a gable roof could provide. A gable roof has more headroom in the center, but not at the sides. Do you need the second floor to accommodate someone standing tall, or will a ceiling height that accommodates a place that is used primarily to lie down and sleep or sit up and play board games be sufficient? For aesthetic and economic reasons, don't build the walls taller than they need to be to give you the desired function. If you have the building skill, then consider adding a dormer in the loft to increase the loft space without making the whole house taller. Hip roofs are

A simple 2x6 ladder leading up to a loft

the worst choice for lofts because the tallest points are in the center of the building, while most lofts are at the edges to make the room feel more open and airy. Keeping that in mind, even a simple shed roof can work if you put the loft on the side with the taller ceiling.

Dormers give this loft a little more light and headroom.

easiest and cheapest to build, but a gable, hip, mansard, or gambrel may appeal more to your sense of style.

|  | Easy to Build | Space for Loft | Best Looking |
|---|---|---|---|
| Hip | * | * | *** |
| Gambrel | * | *** | ** |
| Salt Box | ** | ** | ** |
| Cross Gable | * | ** | *** |
| Gable | ** | ** | ** |
| Flat | *** | * | * |
| Shed | *** | ** | * |
| Mansard | * | *** | ** |

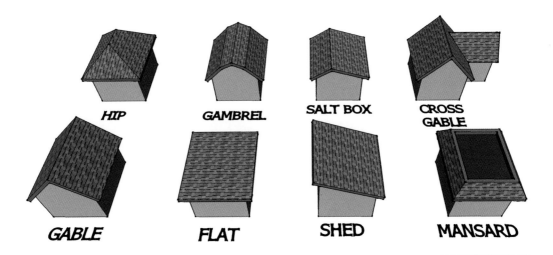

HIP    GAMBREL    SALT BOX    CROSS GABLE

GABLE    FLAT    SHED    MANSARD

Common roof framing options

## OW TO WATERPROOF A TRUNK OR BRANCH

In general home construction, pipes pass up through the roof, and the roofers find a way to keep homes dry. The most common way to do that is with the use of a pipe collar. The pipe collar is pushed down over the pipe and shingles are laid around it. However, in treehouse building, you can't force a pipe collar over the top of the tree and push it down to the roof. What you *can* do is make your own in place as you install the roofing.

A commonly available flashing material is a large truck or tractor tire inner tube. Since the rubber has a curve to it already, you can wrap it around the tree and tap in a nail or screw to hold it into the wood of the tree. Use two to five nails or screws, based on how big the tree is and how many it takes to hold the tube in place. The nails should stick out a couple inches from the tree, because the next step is to wrap a bungee cord around the tree just beneath the nails, which keeps the inner tube snug without girdling the tree. Next, you may use silicone caulk to attempt to seal the inner tube to the tree bark. On large, thick-barked trees, I have sometimes used four

This branch creates two places where a flexible waterproof collar will need to be fashioned in place.

Rubber flashing, fashioned in place, is the best way to keep water out.

full tubes on a truck while working about a ½-inch bead into all of the bark crevices or fissures. The rubber and silicone won't hurt the tree, and putting a few nails in the tree in this manner is inconsequential damage. As long as the tire tube angles down a bit and diverts water over the top of the roofing material, then it keeps water out. You may decide to tack the bottom edge of the rubber down to the roof if the tree moves a lot, but make sure you don't stretch it tight before fastening, because when the tree sways the other way, it might pull the rubber tube and start to ruin your work.

Flashing around branches is tougher than sealing around a trunk going through the roof. Branches move more in the wind, so you need to leave a larger gap in the framing. The

## ALTERNATIVE MATERIALS

If a tractor tire is too hard to find, then you may be able to use EPDM or some other rolled rubber roofing material. I have even used four layers of a heavy-duty brown tarp in a pinch—not as elegant, but the principles are the same. I do not usually go for metal flashing against the tree, because it tends to cause tree bark damage as the tree moves.

...lar must tolerate the movement and cover a wider gap. One hint is to line the hole in the framing with something that the branch can rub against without damage. Good ideas would be rubber, horse stall matting, layers of old carpet, or anything that won't damage bark but will stay in place.

And then, eventually, *realitree* sets in. No roof with a branch or tree trunk passing through it will stay dry forever. The tree gets thicker each year, and the wind moves the tree around in relation to the roof. I like to joke with people at conferences that I can guarantee that the roof will not leak on the day that I finish building it! Eventually, the roof will start to leak and need maintenance. If you are OK with periodic maintenance, then go ahead and give it a try.

# CHAPTER 7

# TREEHOUSE ACCESSORIES

**M**ost of the time you spend building your treehouse will be on the main structure. However, most of the time you spend enjoying your treehouse will be on the various accessories and options that you can add on to the project. I have spent more time napping in my hammock than I ever spent building my treehouse.

Simple hammocks can stretch between two hooks or be easily disconnected when not in use.

## BUCKET AND PULLEY

By far the most requested accessory on a backyard treehouse is the bucket and pulley. The typical configuration is a simple 1:1 pulley with the pulley mounted to a tall railing post or an overhanging tree branch. I like to tie one end of the rope to the bucket and the other end to the railings so that the rope does not slide all the way through the pulley. I have seen kids fill up the bucket with rocks and then run around the tree, up the ladder, out the door, down the porch, and then hoist up the rocks, only to dump the rocks overboard and run down to repeat the process. For a $2 pail, a $4 pulley, and $10 of rope, every treehouse designed for kids should have one of these.

The pulley is attached to an overhead branch so that the rising bucket clears the edge of the railing.

The red pail full of my favorite things

## ROPE SWINGS

All ages of people can enjoy tree swings. They go very well underneath a treehouse or on a nearby branch. This is why swings are the most popular accessory for kids' and adults' treehouses.

## Double Rope Swings

A typical play set swing has two ropes (or chains) that hang down about 18 inches to 36 inches apart. The ropes can be fastened to a structural member of the treehouse, such as a beam or floor joist, or connected to a branch that is close to horizontal. These swing seats are commonly wooden or rubber. The rubber ones come in residential and commercial quality, which affects how long they will last. Commercial swings often have metal inserts that reinforce the attachment holes and are made with thicker

Left: These rustic plank swings use traditional swing-set hardware to attach to the treehouse.
Right: These half-log swing seats are tied with a bowline knot.

material. When you sit in a rubber belt-style seat, the two ropes angle in to fit the outside of your waist. However, with wooden plank seats, the width of the seat is fixed. This is important to note when hanging the two ropes, because you want the distance of the two ropes at the top to be slightly wider than the width of the seat at the bottom. This will make both ropes angle inward slightly, which will limit twisting during normal use. Of course, if a seven-year-old wants his friend to twist him up so he can spin all the way down, causing the seven-year-old to be unable to stand up straight or possibly throw up, then you can install the ropes to angle wider toward the bottom if desired.

When suitable branches are not available, the wire method can work.

## Single Rope Swings

Sometimes called the "monkey swing," these wild rides can go in any direction and be attached up to about 80 feet off the ground. But the wild-and-crazy factor is mostly a function of how tall the swing is and how big a push you get, as the shorter ones can be quite tame. A single rope is attached to a tree branch, and a loop of rope or a round seat with a central hole is tied onto the bottom. You need to have a branch that extends over an open area, because while the swing can move in any direction back and forth, it tends to shift to an elliptical or circular pathway. Running into tree trunks or treehouse support posts can really hurt. The space requirement is

The monkey swing is a weatherproof disk seat that can swing in any direction from a single rope.

the reason these swings don't work particularly well on play sets with the familiar A-frame supports.

**Safety Alert:** Rope does not last forever outdoors. Make sure to use a high-quality synthetic rope and regularly inspect the rope for wear or damage. Serious injury and death happen every year when old ropes break unexpectedly. Never use natural fiber ropes such as manila or hemp outdoors where they can get wet. Always start with a rope that is over 5,000 pounds breaking strength, and preferably over 10,000 pounds, so that it will remain strong enough for a longer time.

The spider swing in single-rope configuration under a treehouse

## Attaching Ropes to Trees

Attaching ropes to a treehouse can be done with off-the-shelf swing hangers or with knots. Hangers either go back and forth for two rope swings, or in all directions for monkey swings, tire swings, and spider swings. Hangers should be attached with heavy-duty galvanized lag bolts, hex bolts, or timber screws. Ideally you want to use fasteners that are ¼ inch in diameter or greater. Remember that pressure-treated wood is corrosive to fasteners, so use hot-dipped galvanized fasteners or other fasteners approved for all types of pressure-treated lumber. You can also skip the hangers and tie a knot around a main beam of the treehouse or other suitably strong attachment spot. I prefer to tie a running bowline knot around the beam with the slip knot area underneath the beam. To improve rope life, sand or round over the sharp edges of the four corners of the beam where the rope will contact over time, and monitor the loop of the bowline knot for wear, as that is where the rope is most likely to eventually break.

There are two main methods for attaching ropes to tree branches. Most arborists have an opinion, but here are the pros and cons of each.

The first method for attaching ropes is to drill a vertical hole through the branch and install a large eyebolt (at least ½ inch but preferably ¾ inch diameter) with the eyelet pointing downward. Ropes are then tied onto the eyebolts. This method does more initial damage to the tree and creates a weak spot where a branch will be more likely to break under heavy load. However, as long as the tree remains healthy, branches can usually respond well to such wounds over time.

The other method is to tie a running bowline around the branch. I have found that this does not girdle tree branches when a large diameter rope such as ¾ inch or greater is used, and a nonconstricting knot is used. The branch can push the rope outward as it grows. The downside is that for trees with thin or soft bark, the slight abrasion can do more damage in the long run than initially installing a bolt.

## Motion of Swings

When attaching to tree branches, it is normal for a swing to move the branch it is attached to, or to even shake the whole tree a little bit. All tree parts are good at dampening movement from wind forces, so as long as the swing doesn't move the branch more severely than the wind does, then seeing the tree dance a little bit with the swing is probably OK. Keep in mind that certain tree species have more brittle branches. I would be happy to swing on a 5-inch-thick oak branch, but I might be concerned about a tulip poplar branch at 5 inches, depending on how far I was attaching the rope away from the trunk. The closer to the trunk, the more reliable the branch is.

When attaching a swing to a treehouse, keep in mind the forces that use of the swing will apply to the platform. For example, if you have a treehouse centered on a single tree, then swinging in a tangential direction will cause the platform to rotate around the tree. In some situations, where the movement is significant, it could cause parts to wear out over time. With other styles of treehouses, diagonal bracing can reduce the amount of movement from the operation of the swing. A traditional swing set frame can be added to the side of a treehouse if there is not room underneath. The A-frame design will help hold the treehouse still when people are swinging back and forth.

## MONKEY BARS

Of the several ways I have seen monkey bars constructed, my favorite for backyard treehouses is the simple screw- or bolt-on handles. They come in four colors, and you can adjust the spacing as desired. We connect these

A monkey bar track is suspended from joists above.

with 3-inch RSS screws. Sometimes you can directly attach the bars to the underside of the floor joists or to a flat 2x4 "track" that you first cross the joists with. But if the track is too high, then you have to drop it down to a safe height for the activity.

## ZIP LINES

Zip lines are a fun addition to a backyard, with or without a treehouse. But there is significant crossover between the outdoorsy imaginative people who want a treehouse and the thrill-seekers who like zip lines. They do seem to go together. In 1990 the movie *Home Alone* showed Kevin making a zip line escape into his treehouse, only to get the drop on the bad guys when they attempted to follow him. That zip line wasn't the safest one I've ever seen, but it certainly had us all thinking that Kevin was a pretty cool

A 700-foot-long zip line is one of our longest residential installations.

little daredevil. So let's talk a bit about how backyard zip lines work, how to install them, and how to minimize risks of injury.

## Slope

In order for the rider to roll down the wire at a fun speed and get most or all of the way to the other end, there must be a negative slope between the wire attachment point at either end of the line. However, in order to avoid crashing at the end, the slope cannot be too steep. For most backyard zip lines, we find that the ideal slope is somewhere around 2 to 3 degrees downward. Longer zip lines must have steeper slopes because of friction on the wire and air resistance. If the slope is less, it makes for a slow ride and may not get the rider all the way to the end. If the slope is steeper, then you need to introduce a braking method to prevent crashing. In order to achieve the proper slope, an elevated platform is usually needed at the start. On flat ground, for a 100-foot zip line, we usually build a launch platform about 6 feet high with a ladder built in. In rare cases, the topography of the land allows a start without a platform, such as if you have a ledge or cliff at the start, and a flat plane or slight bowl-shaped landing area near the end.

## Sag

The zip line wire hangs in what mathematically is called a catenary curve, which to the untrained eye looks like half of an ellipse. However, most of us wanting to install a zip line in our backyards do not want to revisit our textbooks or hire an engineer to run numbers for us. To simplify, you can approximate with trigonometry, which is more accessible to some people, though a little less accurate. The nonmathematical explanation is that a load applied downward on the middle of a zip line wire is magnified by the amount of tension on the wire. The tighter the wire is, the higher the tension when loaded. Therefore, the wire must sag enough or it could break. I know it seems unbelievable that you could break a wire that is 14,400 pounds or more with just the weight of a person, but under some conditions it is possible. When you terminate a wire with cable clamps, 20 percent of the wire strength is lost, so you are down to 11,520 pounds. Next, you should use a safety factor of 5:1, which means that the zip line should be designed to hold five times the expected load. Now you're down to 2,304 pounds. The safety factor will help riders stay safe in the event of shock loading and will compensate over time for strength loss due to wire rope that rusts or becomes worn. I have a tool that measures wire tension, and I have seen some backyard zip lines with over 2,304 pounds of tension on the wire while in use. These wires were obviously very tight and would have been overtightened with a come-along or winch when installed. One way to decrease tension is to introduce more sag into the wire. This might require raising the attachment points at both sides to maintain the proper slope without bottoming out in the middle of the ride. This all may sound very complicated, but short zip lines can usually be figured out by taking a guess, temporarily setting it up, testing with a sandbag or other test weight, making adjustments, and then retesting it until it looks ready for a live human ride.

## Zip Lines and Safety

There is always a risk of injury with zip lines. People are at heights, in motion, and using their judgment. The risks are similar to riding a horse or a mountain bike. There are no codes that currently apply to backyard zip lines. The challenge-course industry has a lot of standards that apply to commercial-use zip lines, which include trained staff to operate each ride and engineers to mathematically justify the safety level and approve each zip line. You can take those steps in your backyard if you wish, but it would be less expensive for you to visit your nearest adventure park and let the professionals handle it. But if you do build your own zip line, here are a few ideas that will keep it as safe as possible.

1. Wear safety harnesses instead of or in addition to telling riders to sit on a seat or hold onto handlebars.

2. Ensure the pathway is clear of branches or other obstacles and the line of sight is sufficient to tell if anything may enter the path while riding. Once you launch, there is no stopping if a car or person enters the pathway.

3. Keep grass and bushes cut underneath, remove rocks, and spread thick wood chips. Pay special attention to these recommendations near launch and landing areas.

4. Treat the zip line with respect for safety as you would a swimming pool, gun, car, or table saw. This means adult supervision, putting the trolley away when not in use, and staying alert and focused while operating the zip line.

Following these recommendations will prevent most accidents from ever happening.

## Materials and Kits

For the first-time zip line installer, it is best to buy a kit that comes with everything you need in one box with instructions. The kits are a good starting point for most situations. My supply company offers a very good backyard kit that comes with instructions and a free telephone support number. When we install zip lines for customers, we normally use slightly different materials so that we can customize the installation and cut the exact amount of wire needed right off a large spool. You can get your own materials, but if you go with new materials, it won't save you money unless you purchase materials in bulk. Be careful with used materials, because you never know the full history of used parts. If a wire rope clip is overtightened, then it could be partially fatigued. If metal is dropped, then it can have very small fractures.

During installation be careful with all of your materials and do not use carabiners or other metal parts that are dropped from a height, especially if they may have landed on rock, concrete, or other hard surfaces.

Immediately retire materials that do not function as new, such as sticky carabiner gates, significantly rusty or worn wire ropes, trolleys that don't roll smoothly, wire rope clip nuts that are stripped, and any parts that are significantly harming the trees by limiting growth or rubbing. Using the right materials and regularly inspecting and replacing them will help keep your zip line safe and fun for years to come.

## CLIMBING WALLS

Small climbing walls are a creative way to ascend a treehouse. If sturdy they also can add some structural support to part of the platform. The rocks can be purchased online, and they are screwed or bolted into a wooden surface. The wooden surface can be ¾-inch plywood or decking boards. I prefer to keep decking boards tight so that fingers cannot get pinched between boards. With plywood, you should apply a solid-color stain or paint to the top and especially the edges to limit weathering; most plywood will not last a year out in the rain without treatment.

When adding a 4-foot-wide climbing wall to the edge of

Typical residential 4-foot-wide climbing wall with grab rope

Over-the-top four-surface, multipitch walls with upgraded climbing holds

a treehouse, we typically build four frame boards that look like rafters or a ship's ladder stringers. Four frame boards will provide support that is 16 inches on center, which is sufficient for normal decking surfaces. At the top of the wall, I like to leave both horizontal rails intact. The lower one makes a nice grab bar, and the upper one adds some safety for people up on top. You can put nets or gates over the openings, but they are challenging to open when you're at the top of the wall trying to get in.

## SLIDES

Slides are a staple for children's treehouses, but the excitement tends to fade around eight years of age, when kids start having more fun climbing *up* the slide as an entrance instead of using it as an escape route. Simple inexpensive slides are usually available in season at big-box retail stores, but these are made for platforms that are 4 or 5 feet high, which is lower than a typical treehouse. A small one-piece slide is a good item to search for secondhand. Many people take down swing sets and throw them away, but the slides have a much longer lifespan, and you may be able to get one free or cheap on a

Back of sectional slide shows side rails and supports.

website like Craigslist. If the treehouse is 8 feet high, you can build a 4-foot ground platform next to it and put two ladders to climb up, and a slide

downward from the ground platform in the middle of the ladders. Another option is a sectional slide, where you buy an entry and exit piece, and then add inserts to get the desired length of the slide. Our store has a sectional slide that installs on two wooden side rails. It only takes about an hour for an experienced person to assemble it, but you may want to plan two to three hours and have a friend help lift it if your slide is going on a platform 8 feet high or taller. Long one-piece metal slides can still be purchased, but they are custom orders, and they cost about three times more than the sectional ones and take at least a couple months to order.

## CARGO NETS

Nets serve many functions with treehouses. You can fashion them into hammocks, use them for climbing, or even fill railings with them. Ordering nets can be a bit confusing, because there are many choices and elements to consider.

For climbing nets, the first decision you need to make is what size material to use. Most custom cargo nets for climbing use ½-inch or ⅝-inch rope that is usually woven and spliced into rectangles, although any shape is possible. Safety nets are typically between ⅛- and ¼-inch material size. The rope is usually white, tan, or black, but other options are sometimes available. The nets can have loops at the ends or just woven boarders. As an installer, it is nice to have loops at the top and bottom of the net. At the top, I can run a 2.5-inch diameter pipe or a 2x4 through the loops to connect the net to the nearest railing posts. At the bottom, I can drive stakes

This cargo net is attached to 6x6 side rails and a pipe at the top as a grab bar.

through the loops into the ground to anchor the net. Some cargo nets are installed onto wooden frames, which keeps them more taut during use. However, these frames need to be sturdy pieces of wood, or they will bend inward with the net. I made the mistake of using 2x8s the first time I tried this, and they looked like bananas after a few climbs. We now use 4x6 as a minimum size for climbing frames.

## Nets and Entrapment

Entrapment is a safety concern for any structure with openings that people can partially fit through. Building codes reflect this danger by requiring that railing spindle spacing be under 4 inches. Small children can fit their hips through a 4-inch space, and their heads can get stuck, possibly leading to death. As a result, no cargo net manufacturer will produce a cargo net with mesh size between 4 inches and 9 inches. The rationale is that if the mesh is 10 inches, then if someone slips through, they will pass completely through instead of becoming entrapped.

## Other Nets

Lately our company has gotten a lot more creative in the many uses for netting. Netting can be used for safety barriers, custom hammocks, and for climbing. The most common safety barrier is as railing fill. Try stapling netting up instead of using wooden spindles on the railing frame for a more nautical or adventurous look. For climbing, there is the typical cargo net,

This stick look is nice, but not long lasting, so netting is added for safety and longevity.

Net installed on framed opening

Climbing structure made with 100 percent netting and rope

Nap time on the Tree Top jobsite

The Greybeard Treehouse at Treehouse World is a triple decker treehouse with all of the walls made of netting. The first level is tricky to navigate as it swings back and forth as you walk, and then you crawl through a cargo net ramp up to the second level. The design is to mimic an old man's face with an islander look to him. The netting bridge attaches to eight other platforms in the children's grove and is next to the tiki-themed birthday party treehouse. Netting is an incredibly versatile material.

The Greybeard Treehouse at Treehouse World uses netting for walls, a ramp, bridge enclosures, and the first floor!

the vertical tunnel climb, and various ramp or layered access levels. My personal favorite is the large group hammock. I like to install them early on a big treehouse project, and then enjoy them at lunch break—sometimes I skip the lunch and the guys wake me up when it's time to work again.

Our nets are typically either tan or black. Tan is the most natural-looking color, but black is more like a shadow. If you want your eye to focus on the netting, get tan, but if you want to see right through it, get black.

## FIRE POLES

Fire poles allow for a quick escape from the trees. They are also possible to climb with sufficient upper-body strength. The authentic brass fire poles are custom made and cost over $3,000. I have found, however, that flag poles will do the job well. Flag poles can be custom ordered at various diameters and lengths. A 3- to 5-inch pole is our most common choice for backyard treehouses. You can also choose a brushed or polished finish. The brushed has more friction, so you don't have to squeeze it as hard to control your descent speed, but some people say that it is too rough on bare skin and prefer the polished. These custom poles are still somewhat pricey, and shipping is high because they are a solid piece. The lowest-cost option is to use a sectional flag pole kit. The kits come with multiple poles about 5 feet long that stack on top of one another. Our kit is a steel kit with a powder-coated finish. I do not recommend the cheapest possible aluminum kits. We used to install them, but we had to replace several of them because they were damaged during use.

Solid piece fire pole with brushed finish

## BRIDGES

For more elaborate treehouse projects, bridges to multiple tree platforms add a lot of fun and make a treehouse feel a lot bigger. The drawbridge can be a good way to join multiple clubhouses or otherwise restrict access. There are basically two styles of bridges that we use between tree platforms: rigid-beam bridges and tension bridges.

Rigid-beam bridges make use of wooden or steel beams that are rigid enough to build a walkway across. The load in the center of the bridge is transferred to each

Ten-foot bridge on residential treehouse

This is a 30-foot bridge to a reservoir overlook.

This 120-foot bridge is for access above river flood stage.

side of the bridge and onto either the platform on each side or directly onto the tree trunks. As with any type of connection between two trees, the bridge must have flexibility to allow the trees to sway. We typically do this either with floating-style brackets directly on the TABs or with a sliding plate on one side of the rigid bridge.

Tension bridges, however, have built-in flexibility because they are made with wire rope, synthetic fiber rope, or chain and therefore can wobble, sink, and lift in response to wind and people walking on top of them. The chief engineering problem is that a significant tension force is created when someone walks on the briidge. This has the effect of pulling inward on whatever the tension members are connected to—either the tree platforms or the trees. The trees are typically a better choice because they

Adventure bridge above waterfall

are stronger. However, with shorter bridges under 20 feet, we have been able to attach them directly to the platforms. We have built larger tension bridges up to 120 feet, but these require very strong attachments to large trees or large ground anchors on either side to handle the tension.

Our favorite bridge style is built on two wire ropes beneath the floor, two rope handrails at the top, and netting to form a basket to fill the sides. We then put wood down to walk across. We offer kits for this style of tension bridge that include materials and instructions. They are available online. Every situation is not the same, however, and it is usually best to call first if you are doing anything unusual or working on a bridge over 20 feet long. Other styles include horizontal treads. Both are safe, but move differently underfoot when walked upon. Whatever style you choose, the materials should be kept lightweight but strong, and the platforms on either side need to be able to support all of the loads.

## LIGHTING

Running electricity to the treehouse is one of the marks of an over-the-top treehouse, but it may not be all that complicated or expensive to achieve. To run permanent power, I prefer to dig a trench toward a support pole or the base of the stairs, and run the power up a pole or stair stringer and into the floor system. From there, it is just like wiring a ground house. An alternate method, if you want to avoid

## BUDGET

The materials and labor budgets should be significantly higher for treehouse projects with bridges. This is due partly to the extra cost of building extra platforms, and partly that bridges take a while to build when working on ladders, scaffolding, and climbing ropes. The higher the bridge, the longer it takes to build.

Battery lanterns are available from camping supply stores.

Conduit runs underneath the net climb so that the trench stays as far from tree roots as possible.

the hard work of trenching or expense of permitting, is to consider the treehouse "temporarily electric." To do this, you wire the treehouse like normal, except that you put a reverse receptacle at the base of the stairs. When you need power, run an extension cord to the stairs and plug the treehouse in. Suddenly you have light switches, a minifridge, and a place to charge devices. I dare say you could even have a television and play poker up there on Saturday nights.

The simplest way to get lighting is with battery lanterns. Lanterns are affordable and perfect for campouts and after-dark adventures. Solar lights also can be installed for additional lighting. Many railing post caps have small built-in solar collectors that will glow for several hours after dark. Larger collectors can be mounted on the south-facing wall of the treehouse, which can power small lamps as needed.

## DECOR

The personalization of treehouses is a big part of what makes them special. Every year we design treehouses around objects that are special to our clients. During a design session in 2005, I asked my clients what kind of treehouse they wanted, and the four-year-old boy went and got his favorite toy, a little boat. So we found some rescue buoys, fish netting, seahorses, and other paraphernalia from the Jersey Shore, and built a boat-shaped treehouse. Another dad had us build a custom gun rack and design the treehouse around it. One woman was grieving for a friend that had just passed away, and so we placed one of her friend's paintings at a focal point in the interior and created a deck facing an amazing view of the mountainside.

Other times the decorations are more of an afterthought, where we build a functional treehouse, and then our clients paint, furnish, and move in. Sometimes we are even invited to the treehouse-warming party! When we have donated projects to the Make-A-Wish Foundation and the Kids Wish Network, the organizations generally reserve a budget to get tables, chairs, toys, video game systems, hammocks, mattresses or sleeping bags, and other accessories to add color and fun to the projects. Those last finishing touches are important and make each treehouse unique and memorable.

# HELP AND RESOURCES

## CLIMBING TREES

Arborists, sport climbers, and construction workers all use different methods to work safely off the ground. I mostly use arborist styles of climbing while building treehouses. I would not argue with you if you choose other methods, but I believe that it is safest to stick to what I know best, and I am a certified arborist.

Ropes can be set in trees with throw lines, poles, or slingshots. The two main divisions in arborist-style climbing are single rope and double rope. The difference is that with double-rope systems, you pass the rope over a reliable branch and tie yourself onto both ends of the rope, ascending and descending with friction knots such as the prusik, tautline hitch, or Blake's hitch. A single-rope system ties one end of the rope to a fixed location, such as the base of a tree, and you climb on the other end.

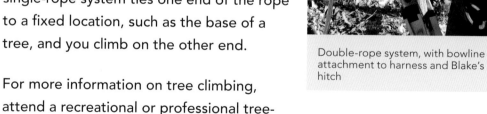

Double-rope system, with bowline attachment to harness and Blake's hitch

For more information on tree climbing, attend a recreational or professional tree-climbing course, learn from an arborist, or use your discretion studying things on the Internet. The relevant safety standard is ANSI Z133 if you want to use today's best practices for tree workers.

# MAINTENANCE AND SAFETY

We all want our treehouses to be safe, long-lasting, and maintenance free. There are some steps you can take to minimize maintenance over time, but no outdoor project that involves wood will last forever without some attention. Here are ideas for increasing the life of your treehouse and keeping it attractive and safe to use over time.

## Wood Protection

The two greatest enemies of dead wood left outside are moisture and sunlight. Moisture is required for wood to rot, so the best way to keep wood from rotting is to keep it dry and allow it to air-dry quickly when it does get wet. Sunlight causes rapid drying on the exposed side of each board, which leads to cupping and checking of wood. The best way to resist the effects of sun and water is to regularly apply a treatment to all wood surfaces.

| | UV Protection | Moisture Protection | Will It Peel? | Durability |
|---|---|---|---|---|
| **Paint** | Great | Great | Yes, eventually | 3 to 15 years |
| **Solid Color Stain** | Good | Great | Resistant | 1 to 8 years |
| **Semitransparent Stain** | OK | Good | Never | 1 to 3 years |
| **Clear Stain or Wood Preservative** | Poor | Good | Never | Up to a year |
| **Oils for Tropical Hardwoods** | Poor | Good | Never | Up to a year |

All paints and stains will last longer when exposure to the elements is less. The exterior decking and railing cap need more maintenance than the siding of a house or fence because horizontal surfaces hold water and snow longer. The sunny side of the treehouse might need a recoat twice as often as the shady side.

**Pro Tip:** It is often easiest to stain/paint materials before they are installed. For example, if you want contrasting colors, it is easier to paint all the wall studs one color before the siding is installed so that there isn't any cutting in. The same goes for the underside of decking boards, the inside of sheathing, or anything that you would rather stain/paint on the ground instead of on a ladder. Having a painting site away from the project also can make cleanup easier and protect the environment.

New lumber can be treated if it is dry. However, most new pressure-treated wood needs at least a year to acclimate before paint has a chance to stick. We sometimes treat new pressure-treated wood with semitransparent or solid color stains right away, as long as it's not excessively wet from the store. If it is, then we can spread the boards out to air-dry for a few days, and then usually they are ready for a coat of stain. Most other lumber, including cedar, redwood, regular dried framing boards (spruce, pine, fir), and plywood, is ready for any type of treatment when new.

## Tree Growth

A treehouse must be adjusted over time to allow space for the tree to grow and sway. As the tree grows, it will eventually come in contact with wood decking, joists, and beams. When contact occurs, the decking should be cut back, and joists and beams should be adjusted outward away from the tree. If you use proper hardware during construction as described in this book, then these outward adjustments are relatively easy to make over the years.

**Pro Tip:** During construction make sure all screw and bolt heads will be accessible to you after construction is complete in case you need to adjust anything.

## Tree Health

The International Society of Arboriculture (isa-arbor.com) is a good place to look up an arborist in your area or to learn more about tree care and related industries.

## ARBORISTS

Even for those of us with a good understanding of tree structure and biology, there are some issues that we miss or notice but can't diagnose. In those cases, it is useful to have a relationship with an expert arborist who can assist in keeping your trees in top shape and treating problems early. If you have an arborist who works on your property, that is probably the right person to consult. If you do not, here are three places to find help:

### International Society of Arboriculture

isa-arbor.com/findanarborist

Look up ISA-certified arborists in your area. This is the level of certification that I currently maintain. My number is PD-2026A. Before hiring someone, make sure that his or her work is primarily "tree care" rather than "tree service." One may have the mind-set of keeping trees alive, while the other makes a living by chopping them up and taking them away. Tree assessments may range from free up to about $250. If you want advice for picking out a tree, but you don't want to pay for any tree care, then I suggest offering to pay something for the advice rather than taking advantage of a professional's time.

## American Society of Consulting Arborists

asca-consultants.org/search

Most of these arborists have a higher level of knowledge and experience than ISA arborists, and tree assessment will therefore likely be more thorough. They generally charge higher consulting fees. I have paid up to about $900 for visual tree-assessment reports. If advanced testing is required, this may cost more, and it is generally only worth it for very high-end luxury residential or large commercial treehouse projects.

## Foresters

eforester.org

(This site is for national certified foresters or to search for foresters in your state or through your state university system.)

A forester may have a broader perspective on the total ecosystem than an arborist, since some suburban arborists "can't see the forest for the trees." So I generally prefer to meet with a forester when assessing a 500-acre site to install a zip line tour. I prefer an arborist when looking at a 1- to 2-acre backyard for a treehouse.

## ENGINEERS AND ARCHITECTS

These experts are often referred to as "design professionals." These professionals are registered or have licenses with every state that they do business in. As such, they have the authority to sign off on plans in order to submit for building permit applications. If you need a permit application, ask the building department at the start which type of professional will be required to certify your plans. If you do not need a permit, however, you may still decide to enlist the services of a design professional. Although the work of engineers and architects can overlap, one general difference is that architects tend to focus more on the creative design process, customer service, and project management, while engineers tend to focus on the math and physics of making a design quantifiably safe.

At Tree Top Builders, we design and build treehouses both with hand sketches and computer-assisted designs, but we work with third-party companies when engineers or architects are required. This is generally the most cost-effective manner of doing business for us due to service and insurance fees.

If you find an engineer who is willing to help you with your project but needs help with the tree attachment process, we are happy to help in a supportive role with a limited design agreement. If you don't have someone local, we have a network with registrations in all fifty states and can bring someone to your project who will do a great job. Here are a few:

**Breckstone Engineering**
breckstonearchitecture.com
Todd Breck has partnered with us on many treehouse projects in recent years.

**Antique Building Materials Co.**
Todd Waltz1001 West Kings Hwy.
Coatesville, PA 19320
(610) 857-1002
antiquebeamsandflooring.com

**Treehouse World**
1442 Phoenixville Pike
West Chester, PA 19380
(484) 329-7853
treehouseworld.com

**Treehouse Supplies**
1444 Phoenixville Pike
West Chester, PA 19380
(610) 701-2458
treehousesupplies.com

**Tree Top Builders, Inc.**
1444 Phoenixville Pike
West Chester, PA 19380
(610) 696-1066
treetopbuilders.net

# GLOSSARY

**Cantilever:** A structural member which extends beyond the point of support. In treehouse building, it usually refers to a beam that projects past the girder or TAB it rests on or a joist that projects past the beam.

**Decurrent tree architecture:** A tree that splits into multiple leading trunks and branches are relatively large.

**Deflection:** A measure of how much "bounciness" a floor system has when loaded. Wood is elastic and springs back, but too much movement can create problems in structures.

**Excurrent tree architecture:** A tree with a dominant central leader and relatively smaller horizontal branches originating radially from the trunk.

**Girdling root:** A root that circles around a tree near its base and constricts the main structural roots that radiate out from the trunk. Girdling roots can come from the same tree or nearby trees.

**Header:** A framing member installed over a wide opening in the common studs such as a window or door opening. The header distributes overhead loads sideways to the jack studs and king studs.

**Jack stud:** A shorter stud which carries load from a header down to the floor.

**King stud:** A full stud (same length as common studs) which adjoins the jack stud and sidecaps a header.

**Root crown clearing:** Removing materials such as soil and rocks away from the base of the tree to inspect for girdling roots or other problems.

**Rough opening:** The size of the opening in a wall frame to allow for fitting of a window or door unit. The rough opening is usually about ½ inch larger than the actual size of a window.

**Shackle:** A U-shaped metal part with a screw-pin.

**Sill plate:** A horizontal framing member forming the bottom of a window rough opening.

**Stair stringer:** The long boards which hold the stair treads and risers. AKA a stair joist. The stair stringer often has triangles cut out to rest treads upon level surfaces.

**Top and bottom plates:** Horizontal framing boards that create an end cap for the wall studs. The bottom plate runs along the floor and the top plate runs along the top of the wall. The top plate is often doubled after the wall frames are installed.

**Turnbuckle:** A long metal chamber that adjusts tension on a wire system.

# INDEX

Note: Page numbers in *italics* indicate plans for treehouses.

real estate, zoning and, 4–5
structure of trees and. *See* trees,
   structure of
time required, 5

## C

cantilevers, 13, 14, 75–76, 169
carpentry
  about: overview of, 9–10
  ground connections and. *See* ground
     connections
  leveling components, 70
  materials. *See* lumber; materials;
     *specific materials*
  structural sense and, 11. *See also* loads
     and loading
  working at height, 101–2
climbing nets, 151
climbing walls, 147–49
codominant stems, 43–44
columns, transferring load to ground,
   16–17
cost. *See* budget

## D

decking. *See* flooring, decks/decking
decor, 161
decurrent tree architecture, 169
definitions
  engineering, 12–13
  glossary of terms, 169–70
deflection
  defined, 13, 169
  maximum, limits, 13–14
  sizing material and, 13–15
doors
  framing around trapdoors, 26–28

unique homemade windows and,
   24–26
double rope swings, 137–38
drawbridges, 156

## E

electricity, lighting and, 159–60
engineering definitions, 12–13
engineers and architects, 166–68
environment, preserving, 32–33
excurrent tree architecture, 43, 169

## F

fasteners
  commonly used, 29
  proper use of, 28–29
  sizes, types, and uses, 28, 29. *See also*
     *specific applications*
fire poles, 155
flag poles, as fire poles, 155
flashing, 108, 111–12, 130–32
floating brackets, 57, 65–66, 89, 95
floating stairs. *See* stairs
flooring, decks/decking
  estimating, buying decking, 69–70
  fasteners for, 110–11
  joist spacing and spans, 20–22, 69
  loading guidelines, 20–22
  outdoor-style, 110–13
  "solid bridging" under, 22
  stiffening bouncy floors, 22
  trapdoors in. *See* trapdoors
  waterproofing tip, 111–13
foresters and arborists, 17, 42, 165–66
Four Trees, 95–99

## G

girdling
  preventing, 64–65, 141
  roots, 45, 169
  wires/wire rope and, 62, 65
Greybeard Treehouse at Treehouse
    World, 154
ground connections
  columns (trees) transferring load to
    ground, 16–17
  post installation and, 18–20
  posts vs. everything else, 65
  trees vs. concrete, 16–17
  using ground support, 17–19
growth of trees
  adjusting treehouse to accommodate,
    164–65
  structure of trees and, 42–43

## H

headers
  defined, 169
  for trapdoors, 27, 69
  for windows, 23, 27
height, working at, 101–2
help and resources, 162–68. *See also*
    professional help
  climbing trees, 162
  cost considerations, 5
  maintenance and safety, 163–65
  tree growth, 164–65
  tree health and arborists, 165–66
  wood protection, 163–64
hollow trees, 44–45
hybrid treehouses, master/slave design
    in, 65–66

## I

insulation
  exterior, 120
  for permanent homes, 121
  wall stud size and, 23

## J

jack, scissor, 109
jack studs, 23, 169
joists
  rim joist tip, 69
  sill plates, 16
  "solid bridging" between, 22
  spacing and spans, 20–22, 69

## K

king studs, 23, 169

## L

labor, cost considerations, 6
ladders
  about: overview of, 113
  building, 113–15
  simplest, 115
  specifications for, 113–15
  wind, ramps and, 117–18
  for working at height, 101–2
lag bolts. *See* bolt attachments
lanterns, battery, 159, 160
leaves, yard, 39
leveling treehouses, 70
lifting materials
  rigging systems for. *See* rigging
  scissor jack for, 109
lighting, 159–60
loads and loading

roofs. *See also* rafters; sheathing
  loading guidelines, 26
  loft space design and, 128
  pitch (steepness), 26
  roofing materials, 126
  styles and functions, 127–29
  styles illustrated, 129
  waterproofing trunks/branches
    penetrating, 130–32
root crown clearing, 46, 169
roots
  girdling, 45, 169
  nutrient uptake and, 38
  structural zone, 45–46
rope swings, 137–42
  attaching ropes to trees, 140–41
  double, 137–38
  motion, forces of, 141–42
  safety alert, 140
  single, 139–40
ropes, for climbing trees, 162
rough openings, 23–24, 27, 169

# S

safety
  climbing trees and, 162
  nets, 151
  rope precautions, 140
  test for walls, 122
  working at height, 101–2
  zip line, 145–46
safety factor, 12–13
scissor jack, 109
shackles, 60, 170
sheathing
  fasteners, 28, 122
  floors and, 112–13
  installing, plans incorporating, 77, 81,
    92, 98

wall loading and, 22–24
Shoe Daisy Treehouse at Treehouse
  World, 108
siding. *See also* walls
  diverting rafter load, 23
  estimating, buying, 70
  fasteners and fastening, 24, 29, 122
  installation tips, 108, 122
  material suggestions, 70
  one layer of, 119–21
  plans using. *See* plans for treehouses
  saving money on, 30–31, 32
  staining, 121
sill plates, 16, 23, 111, 170
single rope swings, 139–40
skylights, framing around, 26–28
slides, 149–50
sliding plates, 92, 117, 157
slings, wrapping with, 63, 64
soil, tree health and, 37–40
square treehouse plan, *78–82*
stains and paints, 163–64
stairs
  about: overview of, 113
  bottom floating, 117–18
  example of stringer layout, 116–17
  floating, 117–18
  principle guiding building of, 115–16
  stringers, 113, 115, 116–17,
    118–19, 170
  top floating, 118–19
  tree movement and, 117–19
  wind, ramps and, 117–18
structural design. *See* ground
  connections; loads and loading
structural of tree. *See* trees, structure of
studs
  estimating, buying, 70
  for framing around windows, 23

# ABOUT THE AUTHOR

Dan Wright is a master carpenter and an ISA-certified arborist. His original company, Tree Top Builders, Inc., has built more than five hundred treehouses (treetopbuilders.net). He also started a retail division, Treehouse Supplies, Inc., which is the leading supplier of treehouse plans, treehouse attachment hardware, and treehouse accessories in the world (treehousesupplies.com). The most recent venture of the company has been the creation and development of Treehouse World,  a world-class treehouse destination with zip lines, unique treehouses, and other outdoor adventures (treehouseworld.com).